50% OFF

Online PECT PreK-4 Prep Course!

Dear Customer,

Thank you for your purchase of this PECT PreK-4 Study Guide. Included with your purchase is **discounted access to our online PECT PreK-4 Prep Course**. Many PECT PreK-4 courses are needlessly expensive and don't deliver enough value. Our course provides the best PECT PreK-4 prep material, and with discounted access, **you only pay half price**.

We have structured our online course to perfectly complement your printed study guide. The PECT PreK-4 Prep Course contains **in-depth lessons** that cover all the most important topics, **40+ video reviews** that explain difficult concepts, over **350 practice questions** to ensure you feel prepared, and more than **600 digital flashcards**, so you can study while you're on the go.

Online PECT PreK-4 Prep Course

Topics Included:

- Child Development, Learning, and Assessment
- Collaboration and Professionalism
- Language and Literacy Development
- Social Studies, Arts, and Humanities
- Mathematics, Science, and Health

Course Features:

- PECT PreK-4 Study Guide
  - Get content that complements our best-selling study guide.
- Full-Length Practice Tests
  - With over 350 practice questions, you can test yourself again and again.
- Mobile Friendly
  - If you need to study on the go, the course is easily accessible from your mobile device.
- PECT PreK-4 Flashcards
  - Our course includes a flashcard mode with over 600 content cards to help you study.

To lock in your discounted access, visit mometrix.com/university/pectprek/ or simply scan this QR code with your smartphone. At the checkout page, enter the discount code: **PECTK50off**

SCAN HERE

If you have any questions or concerns, please contact us at support@mometrix.com.

Mometrix
TEST PREPARATION

PECT

PreK-4 Practice Questions

PECT Practice Tests and Exam Review for the Pennsylvania Educator Certification Tests

Mometrix
TEST PREPARATION

DEAR FUTURE EXAM SUCCESS STORY

First of all, **THANK YOU** for purchasing Mometrix study materials!

Second, congratulations! You are one of the few determined test-takers who are committed to doing whatever it takes to excel on your exam. **You have come to the right place.** We developed these practice tests with one goal in mind: to deliver you the best possible approximation of the questions you will see on test day.

Standardized testing is one of the biggest obstacles on your road to success, which only increases the importance of doing well in the high-pressure, high-stakes environment of test day. Your results on this test could have a significant impact on your future, and these practice tests will give you the repetitions you need to build your familiarity and confidence with the test content and format to help you achieve your full potential on test day.

Your success is our success

We would love to hear from you! If you would like to share the story of your exam success or if you have any questions or comments in regard to our products, please contact us at **800-673-8175** or **support@mometrix.com**.

Thanks again for your business and we wish you continued success!

Sincerely,
The Mometrix Test Preparation Team

Written and edited by the Mometrix Exam Secrets Test Prep Team
Printed in the United States of America

Table of Contents

Practice Test #1

Child Development, Learning, and Assessment

1. A first-grade teacher is planning a lesson focused on recalling the main idea and key details from informational texts. Which of the following strategies should this teacher use to align learning with students' zone of proximal development as they learn this new concept?

a. Flexible grouping
b. Formative assessments
c. Differentiated instruction
d. Scaffolding

2. One of the most important factors influencing the quality of learning and development among young children is:

a. Background knowledge and experiences
b. Adequate health and nutrition
c. Intrinsic motivation
d. Parental involvement in the education program

3. A second-grade teacher is planning a science lesson on the water cycle that will include several unfamiliar vocabulary terms. Based on typical progressions of linguistic development, this teacher can reasonably expect that students can do which of the following when introduced to the new vocabulary?

a. Ask questions about meaning and utilize new terms in various contexts
b. Accurately guess meaning based on context clues
c. Pronounce new, complex vocabulary without difficulty
d. Identify prefixes and suffixes to derive meaning

4. In the art center of a kindergarten classroom, the teacher has included multiple tools of varying sizes, such as pencils, paintbrushes, and crayons. This strategy is likely intended to promote students' development of which of the following?

a. Gross motor skills
b. Artistic expression
c. Fine motor skills
d. Locomotor skills

5. A prekindergarten teacher has just completed a science lesson on changes in seasons and weather conditions. Which of the following strategies would likely best help students internalize this new concept based on their cognitive developmental level?

a. Having students practice writing vocabulary terms associated with seasons and weather patterns
b. Incorporating various types of seasonal clothing into the dramatic play area
c. Make accurate predictions about weather conditions
d. Leading a class discussion on the effects of climate change on weather and seasons

6. A second-grade teacher is planning a unit on place value. Which of the following steps would help this teacher ensure that instruction, learning activities, and classroom assessments throughout the unit are developmentally appropriate and challenging for all students?

a. Reviewing students' standardized assessment scores in mathematics from the previous school year
b. Conducting an interest inventory to determine students' preferred methods of learning
c. Referring to district or state academic standards for expectations regarding student performance in second-grade mathematics
d. Differentiating instructional strategies to appeal to all learning styles

7. In order to establish an inclusive, respectful, and supportive classroom environment, it is important that teachers first do which of the following?

a. Recognize and eliminate personal biases toward other groups
b. Differentiate instruction to appeal to varying learning styles
c. Understand students' learning needs relative to their developmental levels
d. Establish and maintain communication with students' families

8. A second-grade teacher has decorated the classroom with a word wall, labels, a bulletin board, and a class calendar. This teacher has also created a classroom library that includes several leveled texts of varying genres for students to utilize. This is an example of which of the following strategies for promoting the learning and development of language and literacy skills for all students?

a. Providing opportunities for student choice in learning
b. Modifying instruction to align with varying abilities
c. Creating a print-rich environment
d. Scaffolding learning activities

9. A third-grade teacher works with a group of students that have a diverse range of backgrounds, experiences, and needs. At the beginning of the year, this teacher attends back-to-school night, and plans to maintain communication with students' families throughout the year by making phone calls, sending emails, and updating a weekly class newsletter. Which of the following best describes how doing so will benefit this teacher's overall instructional effectiveness?

a. Students will be more inclined to follow classroom expectations.
b. Family members will be able to contribute to curriculum planning.
c. The teacher will easily be able to document interactions with students' families.
d. The teacher will be able to create more culturally, linguistically, and developmentally responsive instruction.

10. Prior to the start of the school year, kindergarteners are given a screening test on various skills across developmental domains. Such an exam is intended to provide teachers with data-based feedback on which of the following?

a. Student readiness and individual learning needs
b. Differences in learning styles
c. The appropriateness of state academic standards
d. Individual students' aptitudes across subject areas

11. After a unit on decimals, a fourth-grade teacher uses a criterion-referenced assessment to evaluate students' mastery of learning objectives. This assessment approach helps this teacher do which of the following?

a. Compare student progress in relation to grade-level peers
b. Determine students' level of prior knowledge
c. Objectively measure student performance to identify individual achievement and learning needs
d. Evaluate student engagement and understanding throughout instruction

12. Which of the following best describes one way that Pennsylvania's English Language Proficiency Standards (ELPS) help teachers design appropriate and effective content assessment for English language learners?

a. Providing teachers with ideas for content-based assessment strategies
b. Emphasizing the importance of students' primary language in English language acquisition
c. Determining the level of linguistic support necessary based on students' level of English language proficiency
d. Finding alternatives to traditional classroom assessments

13. A third-grade teacher uses an analytic rubric while evaluating students' explanatory essays. Doing so helps this teacher avoids which of the following?

a. Taking too long to provide students with feedback
b. Assessment bias
c. Inaccurate scoring
d. Providing irrelevant feedback

14. After completing each unit in social studies, a second-grade teacher typically administers a multiple-choice exam to evaluate student understanding. Which of the following assessment approaches would be more effective in identifying individual needs and supporting the development of all students?

a. Focusing primarily on formative assessments
b. Compiling examples of student work to include in a portfolio
c. Utilizing different assessment strategies throughout instruction
d. Having students self-reflect on their level of understanding

15. Using technological resources for maintaining records of student performance, such as online gradebooks and data spreadsheets, helps teachers do which of the following?

a. Stay current on pedagogical developments in assessment
b. Differentiate instructional strategies to meet students' learning needs
c. Align classroom assessments with state academic standards
d. Efficiently and accurately collect, analyze, and interpret data regarding student performance

16. A first-grade teacher wants to include students' families as active participants in the assessment of their children's learning and development. Which of the following strategies would likely best achieve this goal?

a. Communicating information about curriculum, assignments, and important updates through a class newsletter
b. Providing families with resources to use at home to prepare their children for upcoming assessments
c. Using a variety of communication methods to meet all families' needs
d. Sending students home with weekly progress reports

17. A first-grade teacher works with a group of primarily native Spanish-speaking students, many of whom are identified as English language learners. In the classroom, this teacher incorporates students' native language into instruction by labeling items in both English and Spanish, including Spanish texts in the class library, and teaching Spanish vocabulary words that correspond to daily lessons. Which of the following best describes the benefit of this strategy?

a. Promoting bilingual immersion for all students
b. Creating an inclusive environment that recognizes the importance of students' primary language in English language acquisition
c. Providing English language learners with the opportunity to learn in their preferred language
d. Scaffolding instruction to align with varying levels of English language proficiency

18. A student in a fourth-grade class struggles with reading comprehension and writing. This student reads at a much slower pace than classmates, and when writing, often misspells high-frequency words and writes several letters backwards. This student has been receiving Response to Intervention (RTI) services to improve literacy skills, but the teacher has noticed minimal progress. Based upon this information, the teacher has the professional responsibility to do which of the following?

a. Refer the student for an initial evaluation with the school special education department.
b. Contact the students' parents to address concerns.
c. Consult grade-level colleagues for instructional strategies that may benefit the student.
d. Offer this student extra tutoring sessions before and after school hours.

19. A fourth-grade student with medically diagnosed attention deficit hyperactivity disorder (ADHD) often becomes overwhelmed and struggles to focus on lengthy reading passages. Which of the following accommodations would best support the student's ability to fully engage in reading assignments?

a. Preferential seating toward the front of the room
b. Providing audio recordings of reading passages
c. Reducing the length of reading assignments and providing enlarged font
d. Chunking the texts and providing extra time for processing

20. A fourth-grade student identified as an English language learner has recently enrolled in a new school. Previously, this student moved around frequently in his home country, and as a result, received minimal formal education. Which of the following best explains how this may slow this student's learning of English?

a. The student is not accustomed to attending formal school.
b. The student was not exposed to English at an early age.
c. Minimal formal education resulted in underdeveloped literacy skills in the primary language.
d. Formal education is not valued as highly in the student's culture.

21. A kindergarten teacher has noticed that one student tends to avoid eye contact when speaking, engages in repetitive hand gestures, and becomes agitated by loud noises in the classroom. The student also struggles with various grade-level-appropriate skills, such as grasping writing utensils, using scissors, and zipping a coat. These characteristics may be indicative of which of the following?

a. A learning disability that impacts the development of self-help skills
b. Potential neglect at home
c. A linguistic developmental delay
d. A developmental disorder that affects progression across domains

22. A third-grade teacher works with students of varying needs and learning abilities, including English language learners. For an upcoming math unit on fractions, which of the following instructional approaches would be most effective in making learning accessible to all students?

a. Incorporating digital resources to promote engagement
b. Beginning the new unit by reviewing previously learned material
c. Presenting new information through a variety of mediums
d. Aligning instructional activities with grade-level district academic standards

Collaboration and Professionalism

23. A second-grade student who is typically outgoing has been withdrawn and agitated in class lately. After contacting home, the teacher learned that the student's parents have recently separated. According to the family systems theory, which of the following best explains why this likely caused the student's recent change in behavior?

a. The student experienced negative interactions with parents.
b. There has been disequilibrium in the family unit.
c. The student is spending more time alone.
d. There has been less emphasis on education at home.

24. A third-grade student has recently transferred to a new school. Under the Family Educational Rights and Privacy Act, the new school has the right to request access to which of the following student information?

a. Previous education records
b. Extracurricular activities and community involvement
c. Learning style and preferences
d. Parents' highest level of education

25. The primary purpose of Title I, Part A of the Elementary and Secondary Education Act is to:

a. Provide academic support to students with learning disabilities.
b. Provide additional support to students from low-income families.
c. Fund the development of parent education programs.
d. Establish partnerships between schools and families.

26. A third-grade teacher is having difficulty sustaining students' attention and interest. In which of the following ways might the grade-level department chairperson be able to help this teacher better meet students' needs to promote engagement?

a. Calling parents and guardians to invoke family engagement in the students' education
b. Rewriting classroom procedures and expectations to reduce distractions
c. Offering guidance on instructional strategies, approaches, and activities
d. Providing lesson materials to differentiate instruction

27. A fourth-grade teacher wants to ensure students are aware of their academic progress. The teacher posts students' assessment scores on the classroom bulletin board next to student identification numbers. This method of communicating grades violates which of the following?

a. IDEA
b. ESSA
c. FERPA
d. ESEA

28. A new first-grade teacher works with several English language learners who have varying degrees of proficiency. Each week, she meets with the school ESL teacher to review weekly lesson plans. Which of the following best describes the benefit of this collaboration for promoting learning and development among ELL students?

a. Gaining insight into these students' backgrounds and experiences
b. Developing strategies to integrate students' primary language into instruction
c. Promoting academic achievement while facilitating English language acquisition
d. Learning the difference between academic and social language acquisition

29. Each month, an elementary school hosts a parent-teacher association meeting in which families are invited to discuss the education program. Which of the following best describes how these meetings promote student learning and development?

a. Maintaining communication through a variety of means
b. Ensuring families are aware of classroom expectations
c. Providing families with access to community support resources
d. Establishing a collaborative partnership between the school and students' families

30. A fourth-grade student has recently begun exhibiting at-risk behaviors in class, such as failure to complete or turn in assignments, declining grades, and hostility toward peers. Upon contacting the student's parents, the teacher learned that the family is experiencing homelessness. Which of the following professionals in the school building would be most helpful in connecting this family to the appropriate community support resources?

a. The grade-level vice principal
b. The school special education teacher
c. The school principal
d. The school pupil personnel worker

31. A group of second-grade students informed their teacher that during physical education class, only boys were allowed to participate in a basketball game. Upon learning this, the teacher has the professional responsibility to do which of the following to protect students' rights?

a. Notify the school administration of the students' claims
b. Meet with the physical education teacher to determine whether the claims are true
c. Refer the students to the school guidance counselor
d. Suggest that the administration conduct a walkthrough observation of the next physical education class

32. According to Lev Vygotsky's sociocultural theory, which of the following best describes why a student's culture impacts his or her learning and development?

a. Learning and cognitive development are intrinsic
b. Learning and development occur primarily through interactions with individuals in one's immediate environment
c. Different cultures place varying degrees of emphasis on education
d. Language barriers may impact the rate at which students learn

33. A second-grade teacher works with a diverse group of students and wants to begin the school year by establishing a positive social context for learning. Which of the following strategies would be most effective?

a. Having students complete interest inventories about their learning styles
b. Reviewing students' assessment scores from the previous school year
c. Encouraging students to share elements of their cultural backgrounds with the class
d. Implementing Positive Behavioral Interventions and Supports (PBIS) strategies

34. A second-grade teacher believes she could improve students' learning experience with updated textbooks and new technology equipment in the classroom. Which of the following steps would be most effective in advocating for better resources to meet students' learning needs?

a. Meeting with the school administration to discuss how new learning materials would benefit students
b. Starting a donation fund among grade-level colleagues to pay for new textbooks and technology equipment
c. Asking students' families to provide the new learning materials
d. Consulting the school library and media specialist for suggestions regarding alternatives to new textbooks and technology equipment

35. During a standardized assessment in English language arts, a third-grade student tells the teacher he is unsure how to answer one of the questions. According to Pennsylvania's Code of Professional Practice and Conduct for Educators, she may NOT:

a. Refuse to help the student with the test question
b. Suggest the student skip the test question
c. Implement additional supports at her own discretion
d. Provide unauthorized assistance to the student during the test

36. A new first-grade teacher wants to collaborate with other grade-level educators to develop instructional practices, strategies, and activities to best meet her students' learning needs. Which of the following would be best?

a. Working with the school mentor teacher
b. Enrolling in online classes related to early childhood education
c. Participating in an online community for first-grade educators
d. Attending district in-service meetings

Language and Literacy Development

37. A second-grade teacher is planning a unit on analyzing informational texts. Based on the Pennsylvania English language arts standards for second grade, which of the following activities would best align with expectations for student performance at this grade level?

a. Recognizing and labeling feeling words within the text
b. Answering "who," "what," "how," and "why" questions about the text
c. Making inferences based on the author's use of literary devices
d. Connecting illustrations to the text

38. A first-grade teacher reviews high-frequency sight words with students each day by having them recite the words aloud from the class word wall, trace them on dotted lines, and practice writing the words independently. These strategies are likely intended to develop which of the following skills?

a. Phonemic awareness
b. Text comprehension
c. Orthographic processing
d. Phonological processing

39. Each week, a kindergarten teacher introduces a new short-vowel sound. To practice, the teacher implements letter games that incorporate movement, chooses books to read aloud that focus on the new sound, and has students recite it along with corresponding CVC words. These activities are beneficial in building which of the following emergent literacy skills?

a. Phonics
b. Receptive language
c. Reading comprehension
d. Orthographic processing

40. Which of the following best describes how immersing students in a print-rich environment contributes to language and literacy development?

a. Differentiating literacy instruction to appeal to various learning styles
b. Encouraging students to interact with a variety of literacy materials
c. Providing multiple opportunities for self-selected reading
d. Reflecting students' diversities in literacy instruction

41. A third-grade teacher wants to develop a community of readers by fostering connections between the literacy curriculum and students' lives. Which of the following strategies would best achieve this goal?

a. Offering students a choice in activities related to literacy instruction
b. Providing daily opportunities for self-selected reading
c. Immersing students in a print-rich environment
d. Incorporating literacy materials that reflect students' diversities into the curriculum

42. To practice decoding skills, a first-grade teacher has students clap out each sound of multisyllabic words. Which of the following additional strategies would best promote the development of this skill for children in this age group?

a. Exposing students to new multisyllabic words in a variety of contexts
b. Having students cut and paste letters to form multisyllabic words
c. Using a semantic map to demonstrate the features of new multisyllabic words
d. Having students identify the prefixes and suffixes of multisyllabic words

43. Labeling items throughout the classroom with words and corresponding images is an effective strategy for promoting prekindergarten students' ability to:

a. Understand the purpose of written language
b. Read written text from left to right
c. Describe the connections between pictures and words
d. Identify and name objects

44. A kindergarten teacher has noticed that one student is struggling with sight word recognition and decoding skills, and is beginning to fall behind the rest of the class. The teacher is concerned that this may impede the student's development of reading comprehension skills. Which of the following interventions would be most appropriate in this situation?

a. Providing individual instruction with a reading resource teacher
b. Implementing Response to Intervention (RTI) services
c. Contacting the student's parents to address the concerns
d. Developing an Individualized Education Program (IEP) to address the student's learning needs

45. A fourth-grade teacher is planning a multi-day unit in which students will write a short research essay on a topic of their choosing. Students will first brainstorm topics using a graphic organizer, and, after a demonstration, will gather relevant supporting evidence for their topics using color-coded notecards. Students will then create an outline of their essay and begin a rough draft, which will be peer-edited prior to writing the final version. By incorporating these activities into the unit, the teacher is planning to guide students through which of the following?

a. Strategies for editing writing using language conventions
b. A formative assessment of students' writing skills
c. Foundational steps of the research process
d. How to use transitional words and phrases to manage the sequence of events

46. A third-grade teacher has noticed that a student often skips words or guesses them incorrectly when reading aloud. When writing, the student often uses inventive spelling, particularly for complex words. The student would likely benefit from intervention to develop which of the following skills?

a. Listening responsively to spoken language
b. Initiating and responding appropriately in conversations
c. Irregular sight word recognition
d. Decoding and encoding

47. A kindergarten teacher wants to determine students' readiness for grade-level language arts instruction at the beginning of the school year. Which of the following assessment approaches would likely be most effective?

a. Conducting a screening assessment focused on foundational literacy skills
b. Observing students as they engage in both structured and unstructured play
c. Reviewing students' prekindergarten portfolios
d. Administering a diagnostic exam focused on the first unit of instruction

48. A second-grade teacher gives each student a list of familiar vocabulary words and asks them to circle the ones that are misspelled. In doing so, this teacher is assessing which of the following skills?

a. Word association
b. Phonological processing
c. Phonemic awareness
d. Orthographic processing

49. A prekindergarten teacher has decorated the classroom with brightly colored posters, signs, and charts, and frequently refers to them throughout the school day. This strategy supports the development of which of the following emergent literacy skills?

a. Letter recognition
b. Word association
c. Print awareness
d. Phonological awareness

50. Which of the following words does NOT contain a digraph?

a. Doing
b. Wait
c. Reaching
d. Quit

51. A second-grade teacher is planning a unit in which students will read and analyze a work of grade-level fictional literature. Prior to introducing the text, the teacher administers a reading comprehension preassessment. Which of the following best describes how the teacher can use the feedback from this assessment to plan instruction?

a. Planning activities aligned with students' learning styles
b. Grouping students based on reading ability
c. Choosing texts based on students' interests
d. Planning formative assessments to measure student progress throughout the unit

52. A kindergarten teacher is reviewing CVC words with students using letter tiles. After students read each word aloud, the teacher removes the first letter and asks them to recite the remaining sound. This activity is an example of which of the following instructional strategies to promote phonemic awareness?

a. Phoneme substitution
b. Phoneme isolation
c. Decoding
d. Phoneme deletion

53. A first-grade student often leaves out the ending sounds when reading regular high-frequency sight words aloud. Which of the following strategies would best help this student improve her decoding skills?

a. Having the student practice sounding out words using letter tiles
b. Incorporating rhyming games and songs into instruction
c. Giving the student a list of spelling words to practice each week
d. Having the student trace and practice writing high frequency sight words

54. After reading an informational text, a third-grade teacher has students write a short opinion piece using sentence frames to guide their responses. This strategy is likely intended to develop students' understanding and use of:

a. Nonverbal communication
b. Context clues
c. Academic language
d. High-frequency sight words

55. A kindergarten teacher is planning to introduce students to word families. A beneficial concept to teach first would be:

a. Automaticity
b. Semantics analysis
c. Onset and rime
d. Prosody

56. A second-grade teacher is working with a student individually on reading aloud. While reading from a short passage, the teacher tells the student to follow along with the text using his index finger. This strategy is likely intended to develop which of the following skills?

a. Prosodic reading
b. Accuracy and rate
c. Blending and segmenting
d. Word recognition

57. A first-grade teacher is using direct instruction to introduce multiple-meaning words to students. Which of the following additional strategies would reinforce this concept?

a. Having students complete sentence dictation exercises
b. Displaying new vocabulary in the classroom with corresponding images
c. Having students practice segmenting the new words
d. Implementing word-building activities using letter tiles

58. A third-grade teacher is preparing to introduce an informational text to students. As a prereading strategy, the teacher reads a portion of the text aloud to the class and pauses at unfamiliar vocabulary. The teacher then asks students to identify surrounding words that may indicate examples, synonyms, antonyms, or definitions of the new words. This strategy is likely intended to develop which of the following skills?

a. Contextual analysis
b. Structural analysis
c. Phonological processing
d. Decoding and encoding

59. After having students read an informational text on the life cycle of plants, a third-grade teacher noticed that some individuals struggled to understand key vocabulary in the passage. Which of the following strategies would likely best help these students improve their comprehension?

a. Assigning comprehension questions corresponding to the text
b. Having students complete a KWL chart
c. Demonstrating how to look up unfamiliar vocabulary in the dictionary
d. Having students create a semantic map

60. While reading a work of fictional literature, a third-grade teacher asks students to circle words that describe the main character in order to determine the character's motives throughout the story. This strategy is likely intended to develop which of the following skills?

a. Literal reading comprehension
b. Inferential reading comprehension
c. Critical reading comprehension
d. Evaluative reading comprehension

61. During a writing activity, a kindergarten teacher prompts students to spell unfamiliar words phonetically. This practice encourages students to use which of the following?

a. Orthographic processing skills
b. Inventive spelling
c. Pre-communicative spelling
d. Decoding skills

62. A prekindergarten teacher uses a combination of verbal cues and nonverbal gestures to signal various transitions in the classroom throughout the school day. This strategy is beneficial in developing students' speaking and listening skills because it:

a. Provides multiple means of understanding
b. Aligns communication with students' developmental levels
c. Demonstrates that communication occurs in a variety of ways
d. Strengthens their understanding of parts of speech and types of sentences

63. A third-grade teacher is planning a unit on identifying and writing compound sentences. Which of the following instructional strategies would best support students' understanding of this concept?

a. Creating a word wall with a list of common conjunctions
b. Asking students to identify compound sentences in grade-level reading passages
c. Implementing sentence-dictation exercises
d. Having students practice the concept using sentence-building strips

64. A fourth-grade teacher is planning a unit in which students will write narrative essays, and wants to focus on developing students' ability to establish a clear beginning, middle, and end. Which of the following prewriting strategies would be most effective?

a. Having students complete a story map
b. Demonstrating how to gather supporting evidence
c. Asking students to brainstorm topics for their narratives
d. Conducting a lesson on transitional words and phrases

65. After a reading fluency check, a first-grade teacher has noticed that a student is struggling to distinguish between open and closed syllables when reading aloud. Which of the following interventions would likely best support the student's development of this skill?

a. Reviewing how to blend and segment syllables
b. Having the student sound out words letter by letter
c. Providing direct instruction on the beginning, middle, and final phonemes in words
d. Having the student practice forming words with letter tiles and reading them aloud

66. A kindergarten teacher wants to promote students' ability to retell a fictional story in sequential order. Which of the following activities would be most effective in achieving this goal with students of this age group?

a. Providing students with a story map to fill out as they read
b. Having students sort events from the story using picture cards
c. Modeling how to identify transitional words and phrases in the text
d. Having students arrange sentences from the story in the order in which they happened

Social Studies

67. After completing a unit on continuity and change over time, a second-grade teacher wants to evaluate students' ability to use timelines for recording events. Which of the following assessment approaches would be most effective in achieving this goal with students of this age group?

a. Observing students as they sequence events from a fictional story
b. Assigning students to write a biographical essay about a prominent historical figure
c. Having students create an autobiographical timeline
d. Having students identify past, present, and future events on a classroom calendar

68. A third-grade teacher is planning a unit on the characteristics of different freshwater and saltwater bodies. Which of the following accompanying activities would best connect this topic to social studies?

a. Leading a class discussion on how hurricanes, tsunamis, and floods impact the environment and human activities
b. Having students complete a research project on how proximity to water bodies influenced human settlement patterns
c. Creating a Venn diagram to compare and contrast the characteristics of saltwater and freshwater bodies
d. Instructing students to identify rural, suburban, and urban locations on a map

69. After completing a social studies unit on the election process, a second-grade teacher has students fill out secret ballots to vote on which review game to play before the summative assessment. This strategy promotes students' sense of:

a. Leadership and social responsibility
b. Moral imperative to follow classroom procedures
c. Respect for diverse opinions and perspectives
d. Democratic ideals and civic duties

70. A fourth-grade teacher is planning a lesson in which students will read and interact with a famous speech by Franklin D. Roosevelt. Prior to beginning the unit, the teacher temporarily groups students based on reading ability. This is an example of which of the following strategies for differentiating instruction?

a. Flexible grouping
b. Heterogeneous grouping
c. Student-choice grouping
d. Random grouping

71. At the beginning of each school day, a kindergarten teacher reviews the monthly calendar with students. The teacher labels days of the week as "yesterday," "today," and "tomorrow," and asks students to identify important events throughout the month. This strategy is beneficial in developing students' sense of which foundational concept related to social studies?

a. How to differentiate between fact and opinion about important events
b. Personal responsibility when working with a group
c. Time, continuity, and change
d. The importance of structure and routine to the function of an organization

72. A first-grade teacher has just completed a lesson on cardinal directions. Which of the following instructional activities would be most appropriate for allowing students of this age group to practice using this skill?

a. Using written directions to draw landmarks on a town map
b. Placing pictures of household items in the correct location on a floor plan template
c. Using an online satellite map to locate various physical and man-made landmarks
d. Comparing and contrasting the features of different types of maps

73. A third-grade teacher wants to implement technology into an upcoming lesson to increase students' awareness and understanding of important buildings, monuments, and statues related to Pennsylvania's history. Which of the following online activities would be most effective in achieving this goal?

a. A slideshow presentation focused on major events in Pennsylvania's history
b. A video clip made by a local historian about important buildings, monuments, and statues in Pennsylvania
c. An online flash card game in which students review the names of major cities in Pennsylvania
d. An online scavenger hunt in which students locate and learn about important buildings, monuments, and statues in Pennsylvania

74. A fourth-grade teacher uses a classroom token economy in which students can redeem tickets earned for positive behavior in exchange for various prizes. The most sought-after prizes require more tickets, whereas less desired items cost less. This strategy promotes students' understanding of which of the following concepts?

a. Supply and demand
b. Scarcity and choice
c. Limited resources
d. Profits and losses

Arts and Humanities

75. A kindergarten teacher strives to promote students' creative self-expression by exposing them to a variety of art materials. In the classroom, students have access to artistic materials throughout the school day, and the teacher integrates arts and humanities into multiple subject areas. Which of the following additional strategies would be effective in achieving this goal?

a. Rotating art materials to provide students with a variety of experiences
b. Modeling the appropriate use and care of art materials
c. Practicing vocabulary related to visual arts
d. Asking open-ended questions about students' artwork

76. When teaching the basic elements of visual arts, early childhood educators should demonstrate familiarity with which of the following?

a. Proportion, hue, intensity, and value
b. Pattern, dimension, value, medium, and balance
c. Color, line, shape, form, and texture
d. Primary, secondary, warm, and cool colors

77. While informally observing students during an unstructured art activity, a prekindergarten teacher noticed that one student struggled to grasp crayons, pencils, and markers. Which of the following strategies for differentiation could this teacher implement to meet this student's needs?

a. Offer the student alternative materials to use during art time.
b. Provide direct instruction on how to properly hold art materials.
c. Allow the student extra time to work on art projects.
d. Provide art materials of various sizes.

78. A fourth-grade teacher has assigned an art project in which students will apply their knowledge of acute, right, and obtuse angles to create a realistic drawing of a city. This strategy promotes students' understanding of which of the following concepts?

a. The importance of accuracy when creating artistic representations
b. The connection between mathematics and the arts
c. How to properly scale a drawing to size
d. The relationship between basic elements of the visual arts

79. Each day during music time, a first-grade teacher leads the class in singing songs that incorporate group movement and dance. Which of the following additional learning materials would promote students' sense of spatial and kinesthetic awareness?

a. A variety of musical instruments
b. Props such as hula hoops, ribbons, and sticks
c. A metronome for keeping time
d. Visual examples of various dance movements

80. A kindergarten teacher has just completed a social studies lesson on the role of firefighters, police officers, and emergency service workers in the community. Which of the following activities would best incorporate the arts and humanities to reinforce students' understanding of these roles?

a. Showing students various images of individuals performing these roles
b. Having students create drawings of various service workers in the community
c. Incorporating movement into songs about community service workers
d. Providing clothing, materials, and props for students to act out these roles

81. During an unstructured art activity, a second-grade teacher walks around to informally observe students' progress. The teacher notices that one student is using paints to create a work of art. Which of the following questions should this teacher ask to promote further exploration and inquiry?

a. "What made you think of this idea?"
b. "Why did you choose these colors for your project?"
c. "Why don't you try adding some warmer colors to your project?"
d. "What do you think would happen if you mixed red and blue?"

Mathematics

82. A second-grade teacher is planning a unit on adding and subtracting numbers up to 1,000. Prior to beginning the unit, the teacher administers a diagnostic assessment focused on content and skills from the upcoming unit. Which of the following foundational concepts should this teacher include on the assessment?

a. Comparing three-digit numbers
b. Order of operations
c. Place value
d. Creating and extending patterns

83. A fourth-grade teacher is planning a lesson in which students will use a variety of recycled materials to create a vehicle that can propel itself forward. This teacher is incorporating which of the following into instruction?

a. Academic language
b. Accelerated math
c. Scaffolded instruction
d. The STEAM model

84. For a lesson on basic multiplication facts, a third-grade teacher provides each student with an individual whiteboard and manipulatives. During the lesson, the teacher shows several problems on the board for students to solve using their manipulatives, and asks them to write their answers on the whiteboards to hold up when they're finished. This activity is an example of which of the following formative assessment approaches?

a. Total participation techniques
b. Informal observation
c. Think-pair-share
d. Student self-assessment

85. A prekindergarten teacher provides each student with a set of counting chips as they practice learning to count to ten. As students count each number aloud, the teacher instructs them to move a chip from one side of their desk to the other. This strategy is likely intended to help students do which of the following as they develop this pre-numeracy skill?

a. Name numerals up to ten
b. Compare numbers between one and ten
c. Recognize and identify numerals
d. Keep track of counting

86. A fifth-grade teacher is planning a unit on adding fractions with unlike denominators and wants to incorporate activities that align with students' varying skills, needs, and ability levels. Which of the following strategies would be most effective in scaffolding instruction to achieve this goal?

a. Reviewing flash cards that include problems with varying levels of difficulty
b. Having students play an online game in which they solve increasingly complex problems
c. Providing manipulatives for students to use as they engage in practice activities
d. Implementing total participation techniques to encourage participation

87. A second-grade teacher wants to promote students' ability to tell time to the nearest five minutes using an analog clock. Which of the following strategies would best support students' development of this skill?

a. Showing images of analog clocks corresponding to the time of events on the daily class schedule
b. Using unit cubes to help students learn to skip count by fives and tens
c. Reviewing addition and subtraction skills to help students determine elapsed time
d. Introducing digital clocks first to teach the general concept of telling time

88. A third-grade teacher displays the following word problem on the projector screen:

Sam went to a bake sale with $10.00. At the bake sale, he purchased two cookies for $1.25 each and a muffin for $2.30. Then, he bought a cupcake for his friend Julie for $1.75. How much money did Sam spend in total? How much money does he have left after the bake sale?

Which of the following instructional strategies would best help students solve this problem?

a. Representing the bake sale items Sam purchased on a pictograph
b. Reviewing how to skip count by fives and tens
c. Providing students with pretend paper money and plastic coins
d. Including a word bank with relevant mathematical language

89. In a prekindergarten classroom, the teacher has labeled each station of the play area with a number. Students' desks are also labeled by number, and a number line is posted on the front wall of the room. At the beginning of each school day, the teacher reviews the date on the class calendar and counts how many students are present. These strategies promote students' learning and development of:

a. Cardinality
b. Number sense
c. Sorting and classifying
d. Ordering

90. A kindergarten teacher wants to begin developing students' ability to think algebraically throughout a unit on adding numbers up to ten. Which of the following strategies would be most effective in achieving this goal?

a. Providing both verbal and written directions on how to add numbers up to ten
b. Modeling how to finger count when adding two numbers
c. Introducing expressions concretely, pictorially, then abstractly
d. Demonstrating where the concept of addition is applicable in real-world situations

91. A third-grade student is having difficulty with the notion that fractions represent parts of a whole. Which of the following learning materials would best support the student's understanding of this concept?

a. A geoboard
b. Base-ten blocks
c. Unit cubes
d. Pattern blocks

92. During unstructured play time, a kindergarten teacher asks a group of students in the block area to arrange the blocks from largest to smallest. This is likely intended to promote students' early development of which of the following foundational skills related to mathematics?

a. Measurement
b. Geometric awareness
c. Pattern recognition
d. Sequencing

93. As a group of fourth-grade students work independently to practice solving division problems, the teacher walks around and asks questions to check for understanding. Which of the following questions would best promote the development of students' mathematical communication skills?

a. "What answer did you get for that problem?"
b. "Can you explain how you got this answer?"
c. "What step did you take first to solve that problem?"
d. "What strategy can you use to check your answers?"

94. A third-grade teacher places the following equation on the board and asks students to estimate the answer:

$$143 + 227 + 96 =$$

Students must already have which of the following skills in order to estimate properly?

a. Representing equations in multiple ways
b. Skip counting by fives and tens
c. Comparing three-digit numbers
d. Rounding numbers to the nearest ten and hundred

95. After conducting a survey on students' favorite seasons, a first-grade teacher tallies up responses on the board. Then, the teacher provides students with a bar graph template and instructs them to color in the appropriate number of spaces to correspond with how many students prefer each season. This strategy is likely intended to develop students' understanding of which of the following?

a. When to use estimation versus calculation
b. The fact that changing an object's appearance does not alter the quantity
c. The idea that data can be represented in multiple ways
d. How to make reasonable predictions in math

96. A prekindergarten teacher notices a group of students building a block tower in the play area of the classroom. Which of the following strategies would best promote their sense of geometric awareness during this activity?

a. Prompting the students to guess the height of the tower
b. Having the students create a drawing of their tower before taking it down
c. Asking the students open-ended questions about their process
d. Encouraging the students to build another, identical tower

Science

97. Each week, a kindergarten teacher assigns a different student to be the class weather reporter. This student looks outside and describes the weather for the rest of the class. Afterward, the teacher records the student's daily report on a class weather chart. These activities encourage students to do which of the following?

a. Make observations about their environment to identify patterns and make predictions
b. Identify the effects of climate change on daily weather patterns
c. Predict how animals will adapt to changes in temperature
d. Select appropriate articles of clothing for each type of weather

98. A second-grade class is reading a text on plants and animals that have gone extinct. As they read, students circle clue words using different colors to indicate whether various statements throughout the text are facts or opinions. This strategy begins to develop students' understanding of:

a. How to create a testable hypothesis
b. The connection between language arts and science
c. The importance of verifiable evidence
d. How to analyze and interpret a nonfiction text

99. During a unit on matter and energy, a class of second-grade students will conduct an investigation to determine which method is most effective in changing a solid to a liquid. Prior to beginning the experiment, the teacher wants to develop students' ability to formulate scientific hypotheses. Which of the following strategies would be most effective in achieving this goal?

a. Reviewing the concept of cause and effect
b. Conducting an example experiment for students to observe
c. Having students conduct online research about the properties of matter
d. Providing students with sentence frames to create "if then" statements

100. A fourth-grade teacher is planning a science unit on agricultural systems and wants to integrate elements from the social studies curriculum. Which of the following activities would best demonstrate the connection between these disciplines?

a. Conducting a lesson on the life cycles of plants and animals
b. Having students complete a research project in which they investigate the agricultural practices involved in making their favorite foods
c. Showing video clips on various agricultural systems and practices
d. Demonstrating how geographic location influenced the development of civilizations

101. A third-grade teacher is planning a unit on forces of motion in which students will work in pairs to investigate the speed at which marbles of varying sizes and weights roll down a ramp. Prior to introducing the unit, the teacher administered a diagnostic exam and identified a few students that will likely need additional support. Which of the following strategies should this teacher implement during the investigation portion of the unit to ensure these students can learn effectively?

a. Provide these students with a graphic organizer to fill out during the investigation.
b. Strategically pair these students with others that can provide scaffolding.
c. Check frequently for understanding throughout the investigation.
d. Have these students complete self-reflection activities at the end of each lesson during the unit.

102. A second-grade teacher works with students of varying interests, skills, and abilities. After completing a unit on the life cycle of animals, this teacher plans to use a project-based approach to evaluate overall understanding. How could the teacher best differentiate this assessment to accommodate all students' learning needs?

a. Implementing a flexible deadline for completing the project
b. Allowing students to choose their groups
c. Providing a variety of materials for students to utilize
d. Creating a project menu to allow for student choice

103. In a prekindergarten classroom, students are creating bird feeders using recycled materials and seeds. The teacher plans to hang the feeders outside and allow students to observe as birds come to eat the seeds. This activity is likely intended to introduce which of the following scientific concepts?

a. The life cycle of animals
b. The difference between living and nonliving things
c. The basic needs of animals
d. The fact that animals grow and change over time

104. A kindergarten teacher is planning a unit on changes that can occur in matter. During one of the lessons, the teacher plans to demonstrate that water takes the shape of its container by having students work in groups to observe what happens when water is transferred between a cup, bowl, and tray. This unit and lesson activity support development of students' understanding of which unifying concept related to scientific learning?

a. Constancy and change
b. Form and function
c. Systems and order
d. Measurement and equilibrium

105. A first-grade teacher is preparing a lesson in which students will work in groups to investigate what happens when food coloring is added to different forms of liquids. At each group, the teacher has placed a bin with measuring spoons, cups, a funnel, and a magnifying glass. Providing these items develops students' understanding of:

a. The connection between science and other disciplines
b. How to follow the steps of the scientific method
c. The purpose of scientific tools and when to use them
d. The proper care, handling, and storage of scientific tools

106. A first-grade teacher is planning a unit on genetics, and would like to integrate art into the science curriculum to introduce this concept. Which of the following activities would be most developmentally appropriate for students of this age group?

a. Leading a class nature walk and having students draw the plants they observe
b. Having students create a family tree
c. Playing a matching game in which students match animals with their offspring
d. Having students use clay to create models of different species of animals

107. During a field trip to a local recycling center, a group of kindergarten students learned that mixing recyclable materials prevents some items from getting recycled. To reinforce this concept in the classroom, the teacher should:

a. Have students conduct an experiment to demonstrate the impacts of litter on the environment.
b. Show examples of recyclable and nonrecyclable materials.
c. Assign an art project that incorporates recyclable materials.
d. Place labeled recycle bins in the classroom.

108. During a lesson on seasonal changes, a fourth-grade student asks the teacher why there is less sunlight during the winter months. Which of the following activities could this teacher implement to best help the student investigate and understand this concept?

a. Creating a three-dimensional model of the Earth's revolution around the Sun
b. Building a diorama of the Earth's position in relation to other planets
c. Constructing an outdoor sundial using recycled materials
d. Having the student keep a daily log of sunrise and sunset times

109. A second-grade teacher is planning a project in which students will plant seeds in containers and then cover some of them with plastic bottles that have been cut in half. This activity is likely intended to begin developing students' understanding of which concept related to agriculture?

a. Plants and animals need food to survive.
b. Recycling materials for agricultural purposes helps reduce waste.
c. There is a relationship between the greenhouse effect and food production.
d. Agricultural practices vary depending on the crop.

110. A first-grade teacher is planning a lesson in which students will identify and compare the features of different earth materials, including soil, rock, pebbles, and clay. Which of the following activities would best promote students' sense of inquiry about this concept?

a. Showing students pictures of different types of earth materials
b. Having students conduct online research about the characteristics of different earth materials
c. Asking open-ended questions about why earth materials take different forms
d. Having students search for and identify different earth materials on the school campus

111. A third-grade teacher is conducting a multi-day unit in which students investigate the effects of combining different substances. As they work, students record their thoughts, processes, and observations in a journal. After each class, the teacher reads through students' journals and provides them with feedback to use the next day. This is an example of which of the following assessment approaches?

a. Formative
b. Observation
c. Summative
d. Norm-referenced

Health

112. A first-grade teacher is conducting a lesson on segmenting multisyllabic words. Which of the following activities could this teacher incorporate into the lesson to promote students' gross motor skill development?

a. Having students practice writing multisyllabic words on dotted-line paper
b. Including a song in which students clap and stomp out the syllables of words
c. Having students count syllables on their fingers
d. Implementing a word-building activity using magnetic letter tiles

113. One of the most significant factors that may influence young children's nutrition, physical health, and overall development is:

a. Cultural background
b. Parents' highest level of education
c. Socioeconomic status
d. Genetic history

114. A third-grade teacher is preparing a project in which students will plan a meal consisting of healthy choices from each food group. Prior to beginning this project, the teacher wants to build students' knowledge of the nutritional benefits of consuming a variety of foods. Which of the following activities could this teacher implement to effectively develop their understanding of this concept?

a. A sorting game in which students categorize foods based on their food group
b. Having students explore the MyPlate website
c. A class discussion on why the food pyramid is no longer used
d. Having students keep a log of the foods they eat in a day

115. In a kindergarten classroom, the teacher asks students to cover their hands in glitter and move around the room to shake hands with their peers. By implementing this activity, the teacher most likely intends to promote students' understanding of which of the following concepts?

a. Prosocial behaviors and positive communication skills
b. Environmental factors that can affect health
c. Identifying the signs of illness
d. How quickly germs can spread

116. A first-grade teacher often looks for fun, engaging opportunities to incorporate and encourage movement throughout the curriculum. Also, this teacher often discusses ways she enjoys exercising, and has decorated the classroom with posters that promote healthy lifestyles, exercise, and good nutrition. She is doing which of the following to promote health and physical fitness?

a. Modeling a positive attitude toward health and physical fitness
b. Presenting health and wellness education in a variety of ways
c. Incorporating kinesthetic components into instruction
d. Demonstrating that physical exercise can take place in different contexts

117. While on a class nature walk, a group of first-grade students encountered a bee nest. The teacher directed students away from the nest, and explained that bee nests should be avoided because bee stings could be harmful. This teachable moment helped students understand which of the following concepts?

a. Environmental factors that can impact health and safety
b. Healthy and unhealthy behaviors
c. How to identify harmful substances
d. The importance of following basic safety rules

118. A physical education teacher is planning a fitness assessment for a group of fourth-grade students with a wide range of skills, abilities, and interests. The assessment will include four activity stations to measure students' strength, endurance, flexibility, and agility. Which of the following additional strategies could this teacher use to best differentiate the assessment in order to meet all students' needs?

a. Allow students the option to complete the activities with a partner.
b. Provide multiple activity options at each station.
c. Avoid using formal grading for the assessment.
d. Create a paper-based assessment as an alternative assignment.

119. A second-grade teacher wants to improve students' fine motor skills by developing their ability to utilize tools with control and skill to perform specific tasks. Which of the following activities would be most developmentally appropriate in achieving this goal for students of this age group?

a. Having students practice grasping drinking cups during meal and snack times
b. Implementing activities that require a pincer grasp
c. Encouraging students to practice self-help skills, such as zipping coats and tying shoes
d. Introducing the concept of typing on a keyboard

120. A physical education teacher is preparing a unit on basketball, and plans to differentiate instruction by grouping students based on ability level. Prior to beginning the unit, the teacher has students participate in a skills test and uses a checklist to evaluate their ability to perform gross motor skills related to the sport. This is an example of which type of assessment approach?

a. Diagnostic
b. Formative
c. Summative
d. Observation

121. In a kindergarten classroom, students are threading beads of various sizes onto a string. This is an example of a developmentally appropriate activity for students to practice which of the following perceptual awareness skills?

a. Temporal awareness
b. Pattern recognition
c. Hand-eye coordination
d. Spatial awareness

122. A second-grade teacher has invited an emergency responder into the classroom to speak with students about when and how to make 911 calls in an emergency. Which follow-up activity could best reinforce this concept?

a. Conducting emergency evacuation drills
b. Leading a class discussion to differentiate emergency and non-emergency scenarios
c. Establishing safety rules for the classroom and discussing their purpose
d. Reviewing environmental risk factors that may cause physical harm

123. During a lesson on the dangers of using harmful substances, a third-grade teacher has students role-play several scenarios in which they are offered drugs and alcohol. This activity develops students' ability to do which of the following?

a. Recognize that drugs and alcohol are damaging to overall health.
b. Understand that medicine is intended only to treat illnesses.
c. Practice basic refusal skills in a variety of situations.
d. Identify what constitutes a drug.

124. By second grade, most students can reasonably be expected to perform which of the following tasks in relation to fine motor development?

a. Use knitting needles to create basic patterns
b. Use tools, with assistance to complete classroom jobs
c. Engage in self-help skills independently
d. Practice using a variety of stringed instruments with accuracy

125. Each day, a kindergarten teacher begins class by leading students in a variety of simple yoga poses. This activity supports students' development of:

a. Locomotor skills
b. Fine motor skills
c. Non-locomotor skills
d. Gross motor skills

126. To protect students' physical safety before allowing them to utilize an outdoor playground, teachers must first ensure that all equipment is:

a. Varied to support differences in student ability
b. Used only for structured play activities
c. Accessible to all students
d. Clean, functional, and the appropriate size

Answer Key and Explanations for Test #1

Child Development, Learning, and Assessment

1. D: The zone of proximal development (ZPD) is a concept developed by Lev Vygotsky to refer to one's ability to perform a given task with the assistance of a more experienced or knowledgeable individual. This is the second of three stages of learning outlined by Vygotsky, with the first referring to that which one cannot achieve even with assistance, and the ultimate being what one can do independently. Vygotsky proposed that if individuals are provided with adequate support while in the ZPD, they will ultimately be able to perform new tasks independently. This theory helps teachers understand how to appropriately scaffold instruction to align with students' abilities and provide necessary guidance as they learn new concepts. In this situation, scaffolds such as graphic organizers, visual aids, or chunked reading passages would be effective in supporting students in their ZPD as they learn to recall the main idea and key details of informational texts.

2. B: The quality of health and nutrition significantly impacts nearly all aspects of learning and development among young children. These factors contribute to students' energy levels, ability to focus and sustain attention in class, working memory, and emotional regulation. Further, adequate health and nutrition are necessary for proper long-term cognitive, physical, social, and emotional development. Teaching young children about the importance of nutrition and maintaining a healthy lifestyle establishes a foundation for encouraging healthy choices throughout life. In addition, teachers must know how to recognize when students' health and nutritional needs are not being met so as to provide the appropriate support and resources.

3. A: While individual students acquire language at varying rates, teachers can design effective instruction based upon knowledge of the typical progressions of linguistic development relative to students' age group. By second grade, students generally have an expansive vocabulary of about 10,000 words or more, and can identify unfamiliar terms. Further, children in this age group can typically ask for clarification and participate in discussions on the meaning of new words, and can use them in various contexts. When presenting new vocabulary about the water cycle, this teacher can reasonably expect students to ask questions about the meaning of unfamiliar words and use them in a variety of situations.

4. C: Fine motor skills are purposeful, coordinated small-muscle movements, specifically using the fingers, hands, and wrists. These skills are needed for a variety of daily tasks, so early childhood educators must offer several materials and activities to develop them. While individual children progress at varying rates, most kindergarten students can reasonably be expected to begin using tools such as pencils, crayons, and paintbrushes with a degree of purpose and control. By incorporating these materials of varying sizes into the art section of the classroom, this teacher effectively promotes students' mastery of fine motor skills while recognizing and accommodating individual ability levels.

5. B: Young children learn most effectively through play, it is important that early childhood educators incorporate several structured and unstructured opportunities to do so. Specifically, dramatic play provides a natural, hands-on setting for young children to organize, represent, and understand their learning as it applies to the world around them. After a lesson on changes in seasons and weather conditions, incorporating various types of seasonal clothing into the dramatic play area would best reinforce this new concept. Doing so would strengthen students' personal connections to learning to promote internalization, and help them understand how clothing choices correspond to changes in seasons and weather.

6. C: State and district academic standards give teachers an important framework for reference regarding expectations for student progress relative to their grade level. When planning a unit, referring to these standards helps ensure that instruction, learning activities, and classroom assessments are aligned. Doing so helps teachers plan developmentally appropriate, meaningful, and challenging learning experiences that adequately prepare students for academic success.

7. A: The nature of the classroom atmosphere significantly impacts the overall quality of learning. Students are more likely to achieve academic success when they feel included, respected, and supported in their learning environment. Establishing such a classroom requires that teachers communicate and model appreciation for students' differences. To do so authentically, teachers must first recognize and work to eliminate any personal biases toward other groups. This includes differences in race, religion, culture, and gender, as well as students' abilities. Doing so will help teachers recognize students as individuals, value their diversities, and encourage students to adopt the same sentiment toward one another. In addition to creating an overall welcoming environment, eliminating personal biases allows teachers to design more effective instruction aligned with students' individual needs to provide a challenging and educationally focused learning experience.

8. C: Print-rich environments promote language and literacy skill development among young children of all proficiency levels, including English language learners and students with learning disabilities. Such an environment exposes students to and encourages them to interact with a variety of print materials, promoting acquisition and retention while demonstrating the applications of literacy in daily life. Further, a print-rich environment aligns learning with students' individual needs, as teachers can provide materials to accommodate a wide range of skill levels. By incorporating a word wall, labels, bulletin board, and calendar, as well as a classroom library with leveled texts, this teacher effectively creates a print-rich environment that is accessible and enriching for all students.

9. D: Establishing and maintaining frequent communication with students' families is essential to planning instruction that is responsive to all students' backgrounds, experiences, and needs. Doing so creates the sentiment that family members are considered equal participants in the education program, and encourages them to share information relevant to their children's needs to help teachers plan more effective instruction. Communicating with students' families provides teachers with valuable insight into the diverse range of cultures, languages, beliefs, and individual abilities that exist within their classroom. By attending back-to-school night and maintaining communication with family members through a variety of means, this teacher will gain a greater understanding of students' needs to create more developmentally, linguistically, and culturally responsive instruction.

10. A: Screening tests are typically administered prior to the beginning of the school year to determine students' level of overall readiness for learning the grade-level curriculum. These tests measure students' abilities across developmental domains, and give teachers data-based feedback to make informed instructional decisions throughout the school year. Screening tests allow teachers to identify individual learning needs and implement appropriate instructional strategies, supports, and accommodations to ensure all students can learn effectively.

11. C: Criterion-referenced assessments are used to evaluate individual student progress in relation to a set of predetermined standards. These assessments typically have a set score that students must earn to indicate mastery of learning objectives. This approach helps prevent assessment bias, as it provides teachers with objective and data-based—and therefore, more accurate—feedback on student achievement. Criterion-referenced assessments allow teachers to identify individual student learning needs to adjust instructional strategies, practices, and supports as necessary, as well as determine the need for potential remediation.

12. C: The Pennsylvania English Language Proficiency Standards for English language learners PreK-12 outline performance indicators for ELL students at varying stages of language acquisition. These standards provide teachers with a framework for reference regarding expectations for student performance, as well as strategies for linguistic support relative to proficiency level. Referring to these standards is integral to planning appropriate and equitable content assessments for ELLs that promote English language acquisition while providing the degree of linguistic support necessary to facilitate achievement of academic standards.

13. B: Teachers have the ethical and professional responsibility to provide a fair assessment of students' academic progress. As such, it is important to maintain impartiality when evaluating students' work. This includes avoiding bias regarding culture, race, gender, or skill level, as well as any preconceived assumptions about individual students' abilities. However, at times, teachers may inadvertently experience unconscious bias that may impact their ability to provide an objective assessment. An effective strategy for avoiding assessment bias—particularly when assignments, such as essays, lend themselves to subjectivity—is to use a rubric with predetermined performance indicators. Specifically, an analytic rubric allows teachers to numerically evaluate student work in relation to several criteria, helping to provide a fair, accurate, and objective assessment.

14. C: Young children learn and demonstrate understanding in multiple ways. As such, it is important to utilize multiple performance indicators to measure student progress toward achieving learning objectives. This includes administering assessments at all stages of the learning process to evaluate student understanding. Doing so gives teachers more accurate, comprehensive feedback regarding individual learning needs, letting them adjust instructional strategies, activities, and supports as necessary to promote development for all students.

15. D: Teachers have the professional responsibility to establish and frequently maintain records of students' progress toward achieving academic standards. Utilizing technological resources, such as online gradebooks or data spreadsheets, is highly beneficial in increasing the efficiency and accuracy of this process. Such tools allow teachers to quantify student performance, thus allowing for an objective analysis and interpretation of data. This provides teachers with an accurate representation of student progress and individual needs so they can adjust instruction as necessary and implement appropriate supports to promote learning and development for all students.

16. B: Establishing, developing, and sustaining productive assessment partnerships with families enhances the overall learning experience and student achievement. To do so, teachers must include family members as equal and active participants in the assessment process. Often, family members are unsure how to contribute to their children's learning and development. By providing resources to utilize at home, such as study guides or review materials for upcoming assessments, teachers help foster the sense of inclusion necessary for an effective partnership.

17. B: Incorporating students' cultural and linguistic diversities into instruction is an important part of creating an inclusive environment in which all students feel safe and supported to engage in learning. For ELL students specifically, this strategy also fosters positive attitudes toward learning English, as it communicates that their primary language is valued and respected in the classroom. Further, incorporating students' native language into instruction promotes English language acquisition, as many foundational literacy skills from one's first language are often transferable to subsequent languages.

18. A: Under the Individuals with Disabilities Education Act (IDEA), teachers that suspect a student may have a learning disability are required to refer the student for an initial evaluation to determine the need for special education services. Doing so is integral to creating an equitable environment in which all students receive the necessary support to learn effectively. In this situation, the fact that the student in question continues to struggle with reading comprehension and writing skills despite receiving RTI services may be indicative of a potential learning disability. Upon noticing the student's lack of progress, this teacher would have the professional responsibility to refer the student for an initial evaluation with the school special education department.

19. D: Students with learning disabilities often require special accommodations to support their individual needs. Accommodations typically do not alter what the student is expected to learn, but facilitate their ability to do so effectively in an equitable environment. Students diagnosed with attention deficit hyperactivity disorder (ADHD) often struggle to focus in class, and may easily become overwhelmed by lengthy assignments. Chunking long reading passages into smaller, more manageable parts, and giving extra time for processing, would help this student sustain attention while reducing feelings of being overwhelmed. These accommodations would ensure that the student is provided with the support necessary to fully engage in learning without reducing academic expectations.

20. C: The degree of literacy skill development in the primary language contributes significantly to the rate of second-language acquisition. Many foundational literacy concepts are transferable from the primary language to subsequent ones, so those with strong skills in this area typically experience greater success and accelerated proficiency development when learning a second language. Since this student received minimal previous formal education, his literacy skills in the primary language are likely underdeveloped, which will likely hinder English language acquisition.

21. D: While all students progress at individual rates, certain atypical patterns may be indicative of a developmental delay. In this situation, the student's symptoms are characteristic of autism spectrum disorder (ASD). This is a developmental condition that can cause a range of delays across domains. Upon noticing that this student displays atypical behaviors, the teacher must refer the student for an initial evaluation to determine the need for special education services. Doing so will help ensure that this student receives the support necessary to learn effectively.

22. C: Applying universal design principles to instruction helps ensure that learning opportunities are equitable and accessible to all students, including those with learning disabilities and those who are English language learners. This approach emphasizes the importance of implementing various methods for engagement, representation, action, and expression of information to meet students' diverse needs in the classroom. In this situation, the teacher could incorporate universal design principles by introducing the new unit on fractions through a variety of mediums. This could be achieved by incorporating such accommodations as visual representations, audio and video clips, and assistive technology as necessary. Doing so would create an inclusive classroom environment in which all student needs are met to promote success in learning.

Collaboration and Professionalism

23. B: The family systems theory states that the family exists as a cohesive unit that strives to achieve equilibrium through the interactions, relationships, and dynamics of the individuals within it. According to this theory, family members directly influence one another, and a sudden shift in dynamics will cause disequilibrium that may worsen their behavior. In this situation, the separation of the student's parents disrupted the dynamics of the family system. As seen through the lens of the family systems theory, this event caused disequilibrium, which caused the change in the student's behavior.

24. A: According to the Family Educational Rights and Privacy Act (FERPA), schools may not disclose information related to students' education records without written permission from the student's parents, guardians, or legal caregivers. This extends to the student's academic, medical, and behavior records, as well as any other personally identifiable information. However, in certain situations—such as when the student enrolls in a new school—schools may release this information without prior consent from the student's designated caregivers. Upon transfer, the new school has the right to request access to the student's previous education records.

25. B: Title I, Part A is a federally funded program intended to help close the achievement gap for economically disadvantaged students. This program allocates more financial assistance to schools with a high percentage of students from low-income households to provide the support necessary to facilitate equitable learning opportunities. Funds may be used to provide learning materials and resources, additional staff, intervention programs, and staff development opportunities. In addition, Title I funds may be used to give families access to resources and education to further support their children's learning and development.

26. C: Each professional in the school building serves an important role in meeting students' learning needs. Consulting and collaborating with these professionals is essential to a positive, productive environment that fosters student learning and development. Department chairs act as leaders among their grade-level or subject-area colleagues. These experienced individuals are valuable resources for their team, as they can offer suggestions, resources, and mentoring on ways to improve one's teaching practice. By consulting the department chair, this teacher can gain insight into effective instructional strategies, approaches, and activities to more effectively meet their students' diverse needs and promote engagement in the classroom.

27. C: Teachers have the legal and professional responsibility to protect the confidentiality of their students. According to the Family Educational Rights and Privacy Act (FERPA), any information related to students' education records, including personally identifiable information, may only be disclosed to parents, guardians, or legal caregivers. In education, personally identifiable information refers to anything that may reveal students' identities, such as names, birth dates, or student identification numbers. In this situation, the teacher reveals both academic records and personally identifiable information by displaying students' assessment scores next to their identification numbers, violating their right to privacy under FERPA.

28. C: Collaborating with other professionals in the school building helps teachers develop effective instructional strategies, approaches, and supports that meet students' diverse needs to promote learning and development. The English as a second language (ESL) specialist works with students whose native language is not English. These professionals are familiar with the nuances of second language acquisition, as well as the needs and abilities of individual English language learners in the school building. The ESL specialist can offer guidance on which linguistic supports will best promote student learning, as well as strategies for incorporating students' language objectives into instruction. By reviewing weekly lesson plans with the school ESL specialist, this teacher can effectively develop and implement strategies for supporting English language acquisition among her ELL students while providing the supports necessary to facilitate academic achievement.

29. D: Students achieve greater academic success when schools and families work together to promote learning and development. It is important to provide frequent opportunities for schools and families to collaborate as equal partners in the education program. Doing so communicates the sentiment that their contributions are valued, encouraging further participation in their children's learning. Holding monthly parent-teacher association meetings provides families with the space to meaningfully share thoughts, ideas, and concerns, and contribute to decisions related to the education program, fostering a positive, collaborative partnership that enhances students' overall learning experience.

30. D: Connecting families to the appropriate community support resources is necessary to ensure students' needs are met for successful learning and development. Schools typically have a pupil personnel worker (PPW) on staff to address and provide support for circumstances that may impede students' ability to learn. These professionals act as liaisons between schools, families, and the community, and can link families to a range of community support resources to address a variety of needs. In this situation, the school PPW could help direct this family toward resources such as social service programs related to homelessness, food banks, and counseling for the student and family.

31. A: Under federal law, teachers have the legal and professional responsibility to ensure all students receive fair and equal access to learning opportunities. Schools may not discriminate against students for any reason, including race, ethnicity, religion, gender, or sexual orientation. Based on the claims of these students, the physical education teacher may be discriminating against the female students in class by not allowing them to participate in basketball games. Upon hearing this information, this teacher must report the claims to the school administration. Doing so will allow the administration to investigate and properly address the issue, protecting students' right to learn.

32. B: Lev Vygotsky proposed that learning and development occur through interactions with individuals in one's immediate environment. For young children, therefore, most early learning experiences take place within the family and community setting prior to beginning school. As values, behaviors, beliefs, and interactions vary among cultures, the nature of learning and development among children will also differ. Teachers must be aware of these differences, as well as the role of family and culture in learning and development, so as to design cross-culturally competent instruction.

33. D: The social context of the classroom significantly impacts students' attitudes toward learning and overall achievement. Teachers must make efforts to ensure that all interactions, behaviors, and relationships in the classroom are positive, respectful, and focused on productive learning. Implementing Positive Behavioral Interventions and Supports (PBIS) in the classroom is an effective strategy for establishing such a social context. This three-tiered framework is intended to promote desired behavior among students through increasingly intensive interventions and supports. First-tier strategies are typically applied to all students, such as implementing classroom behavioral expectations, praising positive behavior, and implementing reward systems. Second-tier interventions support small groups of students, and may include communication with students' families, implementing a daily check-in system, or revising behavioral expectations. Tier-three interventions focus on individual students that continuously exhibit negative behaviors, and include specialized supports such as counseling, behavior contracts, and behavior intervention plans (BIPs). In this situation, the teacher should first implement tier-one supports, such as praising desired behavior and creating classroom expectations, to establish a positive social context at the beginning of the year. This teacher should consistently implement these strategies throughout the year to maintain a positive, productive learning environment.

34. A: Advocating for students' needs is integral to ensuring they have the resources and support necessary for academic achievement. This includes ensuring that all students have the materials and equipment necessary to reach their full learning potential. To best advocate for better textbooks and technology equipment in this situation, the teacher should begin by meeting with the school administration to discuss her concerns and ideas. In doing so, the teacher can explain why the new learning materials would benefit students, and potentially influence decision-making on budgeting for the education program.

35. D: Standardized assessments are intended to provide objective feedback regarding students' progress in reaching state and district academic standards. The results of these tests are used for a variety of purposes related to the education program, such as curriculum planning, student placement, and resource allocation. Teachers therefore have the ethical responsibility to adhere to their state and district's code of conduct regarding practices related to standardized assessments. According to Pennsylvania's Code of Professional Practice and Conduct for Educators, teachers may not provide unauthorized assistance to students during these assessments. In this situation, the teacher may be able to reread assessment directions aloud, but may not offer any information that would allow students to infer the answer to specific test questions.

36. C: Collaboration with other grade-level colleagues is essential to continuously developing one's pedagogical knowledge and skills. Numerous online resources are available to facilitate such collaboration, such as online communities focused on teaching specific grade levels. In this space, teachers from different locations and levels of experience can interact to share thoughts, ideas, and experiences within the realm of education. By participating in an online community of first-grade educators, this teacher can build on others' diverse range of experiences and learn best practices, instructional strategies, and activities for meeting students' learning needs.

Language and Literacy Development

37. B: The Pennsylvania PreK-4 learning standards for English language arts outline expectations for student performance at each grade level, and should be used as a framework for planning instruction, lesson activities, and classroom assessments. According to these standards, second-grade students can reasonably be expected to use details from a grade-level informational text to answer specific questions. This includes correctly responding to "who," "what," "how," and "why" questions.

38. C: Orthographic processing skills are the ability to recognize and recall written words. These skills are necessary for the development of reading and writing fluency, as they are foundational for decoding both familiar and unfamiliar words, as well as using proper spelling and punctuation conventions. Activities to promote orthographic processing skills should include multiple opportunities for students to use and visualize words in written form, such as by tracing and writing sight words and reciting them aloud from a word wall. Such activities help students internalize the spelling, pronunciation, and meaning of new vocabulary, thus building writing and reading comprehension skills.

39. A: Explicit phonics instruction is essential for developing foundational reading and writing literacy skills among young children. Phonics is the ability to recognize which sounds are made by individual letters or groups of letters, and is therefore necessary to decode, comprehend, and produce entire written words. Many beginner-level sight words, such as consonant-vowel-consonant (CVC) words, are easy to spell and include short-vowel sounds, so using them to introduce phonics promotes word recognition and retention. Further, reviewing short-vowel sounds through varied repetition and kinesthetic activities helps young children internalize the concept of phonics to build literacy skills.

40. B: Immersing young children in a print-rich classroom environment exposes them to a variety of language and literacy materials to promote early skill development. Such an environment may include such components as a vocabulary word wall, labels, bulletin boards, a writing center, and a classroom library containing texts of varying genres and levels of complexity. In a print-rich classroom, students are encouraged to interact with literacy materials in a variety of contexts. This helps to build foundational knowledge while demonstrating the prevalence of literacy in everyday life, strengthening students' connections to learning and fostering positive attitudes toward literacy.

41. D: Students achieve more when they are able to make personal connections to the curriculum through relevant, meaningful learning experiences. For literacy instruction specifically, this includes incorporating materials into the curriculum that reflect students' diverse backgrounds, cultures, and experiences. Doing so helps to create an inclusive learning environment that contributes to developing a community of readers. When students can see themselves represented in literacy materials, they are able to establish personal connections, fostering positive attitudes and encouraging active participation in learning.

42. B: Decoding is the ability to recognize and pronounce written language by correctly sounding out the letters within words. Selecting age-appropriate learning materials is important in designing instruction that builds this emergent literacy skill to ultimately promote reading comprehension and fluency. Young children learn best through active, hands-on learning experiences, implementing kinesthetic activities in literacy instruction helps to strengthen connections and increase retention. In this situation, having students cut and paste letters to create multisyllabic words allows them to physically interact with learning materials, promoting their understanding of letter-sound relationships to build decoding skills.

43. D: Learning to name and identify objects is an essential component of speech and language development. This concept should be integrated throughout all areas of the early childhood curriculum. Strategies that promote receptive language skills, such as labeling items in the classroom with words and corresponding images, help young children learn the names of objects around them. This provides consistent exposure to vocabulary in a variety of contexts to reinforce understanding and increase retention.

44. B: Response to Intervention (RTI) is a three-tiered model intended to provide students that struggle in a particular content area with additional support. Each tier consists of increasingly intensive services designed to develop students' skills to a grade-appropriate level. Tier-one RTI services are generally applied to all students to promote universal understanding and achievement. Students that continue to have difficulty are typically referred for tier-two RTI services, in which they receive small-group instruction outside the classroom to develop their skills in the given subject area. Tier-three services are directed toward individual students in need of significant support. In this situation, the student likely has not responded to the tier-one interventions applied to the whole class, and therefore would benefit from receiving tier-two RTI services.

45. C: Guiding students through the foundational steps of the research process should begin in early elementary school. Doing so promotes writing skill development while establishing a foundation for success across content areas. In this situation, the teacher plans to guide students through the steps of the research process with each activity. Having students brainstorm topics will help them narrow their essay's focus. Demonstrating how to gather evidence shows students how to effectively support their writing topics with relevant information. Assigning students to create outlines prior to beginning rough drafts will help them organize their writing, while peer-editing will help them refine it. These activities for each stage of the research process will help students produce clear, coherent, and organized essays while promoting writing skill development.

46. D: In phonics, decoding refers to one's ability to recognize and correctly pronounce sounds produced by written letters and words. Encoding refers to one's ability to identify and produce written letters and words to correspond to the sounds of spoken language. These skills are reciprocal, and both are imperative for literacy development across domains, as they directly contribute to students' reading comprehension, writing, and oral language abilities. In this situation, the student shows deficiencies with both decoding and encoding, and therefore would benefit from more support to develop these skills.

47. A: Screening assessments are typically administered at the beginning of the school year to determine students' level of readiness to participate in grade-level instruction in a particular content area. These assessments provide teachers with valuable feedback on students' prior knowledge, abilities, and skills so teachers can prepare instruction that aligns with their developmental levels and individual needs. Screening assessments can be conducted either formally or informally, and generally include the curriculum that will be covered throughout the school year. In this situation, conducting a universal screening test focused on foundational literacy skills will help this teacher select appropriate learning materials, implement necessary supports, and differentiate instruction to promote success for all students.

48. D: Orthographic processing skills encompass the ability to recognize and recall written words, as well as implement conventions related to writing, including spelling, punctuation, and capitalization. Students with strong orthographic processing skills are able to visually identify when a word is spelled incorrectly because of their understanding of the parts of words. In this situation, by asking students to circle misspelled words from a list of familiar vocabulary, the teacher is assessing students' orthographic processing skills in relation to writing conventions.

49. C: Print awareness is the understanding of the prevalence of printed language in everyday life, as well as the recognition that printed words and letters convey meaning. Understanding this basic concept of print is foundational in emergent literacy skill development, so it must be emphasized in the early childhood classroom. Surrounding young children with multiple examples of environmental print, such as posters, signs, and charts, demonstrates the existence and purpose of printed language to begin building print awareness.

50. A: A digraph is the combination of two letters to create a single phoneme. These combinations may consist of vowels, consonants, or a combination of both, but must only produce one syllable. Digraphs are common in English, so identifying and recognizing the sounds they produce is fundamental in building word recognition and reading comprehension skills. Common examples of digraphs include "ch," "qu," "ai," "sh," and "th." While "oi" can also be a digraph in some cases, in a word such as "doing," the letters "o" and "i" are pronounced as two syllables, so it is not a digraph.

51. B: Diagnostic assessments are typically administered prior to a new unit of instruction. These assessments can take several forms, such as preassessments, anticipation guides, or surveys, and are intended to provide teachers with feedback on students' background knowledge, abilities, and level of understanding in relation to the upcoming unit. Teachers can use this feedback to guide the planning process, as it allows them to identify areas of student need to implement appropriate strategies, supports, and accommodations. For English language arts, this can include using preassessment data to group students based on reading ability. Doing so will help the teacher scaffold instruction to ensure learning aligns with students' needs to be successful throughout the unit.

52. D: Phoneme deletion is an instructional activity in which students practice sounding out parts of words after one phoneme, or sound, has been removed. This strategy develops students' sense of phonemic awareness, or the ability to distinguish individual sounds in spoken words or parts of words. Building phonemic awareness is foundational for emergent literacy skill development, as it contributes to phonological awareness, which is the ability to differentiate and understand words and sounds in spoken language as a whole.

53. A: The ability to isolate individual phonemes is essential to building the degree of phonemic awareness necessary for oral language and reading comprehension development. While activities such as rhyming games, chants, and songs help young children acquire this skill, such activities often present new words in their entirety, which proves difficult for some students. When decoding regular high-frequency sight words, students may recognize and correctly pronounce the root of the word, but often ignore modifiers such as prefixes or suffixes, leading to errors in pronunciation. Having struggling students practice sounding out words using letter tiles lets them visualize and physically manipulate each letter, strengthening their understanding of letter-sound relationships.

54. C: Academic language is language used primarily in the realm of education. Its complexity and content-specific nature often make it difficult for young children to acquire, comprehend, and use correctly. However, academic language is a necessary component to literacy skill development and achievement across content areas. Sentence frames are an effective tool for guiding students as they learn to use this unfamiliar vocabulary. This strategy contextualizes and scaffolds learning by prompting students to fill in blanks as they craft written responses, supporting their understanding of how to use academic language.

55. C: Word families are words that are spelled and pronounced similarly. For example, the words "brain," "rain," "stain," and "train" all share the "-ain" ending, and therefore belong to the same word family. Introducing word families using the concept of onset and rime—the beginning and ending sounds of a syllable—familiarizes students with the different parts of words. The onset is the initial consonant that begins the syllable, and the rime consists of the remaining vowels and consonants. Teaching this concept first contributes to developing the phonological awareness skills necessary for decoding written language. Doing so helps students identify words in the same word family while promoting vocabulary acquisition, word recognition, and ultimately, reading comprehension skills.

56. B: Accuracy and rate are essential components to building reading fluency. Accuracy is the ability to read and comprehend text with minimal errors, and rate is the speed at which one reads. Typically, as accuracy improves, rate also increases. Having students physically track text using their finger when reading is an effective strategy for developing both these skills. Doing so enhances students' ability to focus on individual words as they read while incorporating a kinesthetic element to strengthen connections as they develop reading comprehension skills.

57. B: Developing students' range of vocabulary is essential to building reading comprehension skills. This includes teaching students that some words in English may have multiple meanings. Homonyms are words that are spelled and pronounced the same, but have different meanings, such as "right," "left," "bat," and "well." Providing consistent reminders of the various meanings of such words helps students internalize this difficult concept to promote retention and deepen their understanding of new vocabulary. After introducing homonyms to students through direct instruction, displaying the new vocabulary with corresponding images would give students a visual reference to reinforce the multiple meanings of these words.

58. A: Contextual analysis skills, or the ability to look for clues within a text to decipher the meaning of unfamiliar words, are essential to vocabulary acquisition and reading comprehension. Examples of context clues include synonyms, antonyms, examples, or definitions that are embedded throughout the text and indicate the meaning of the new word. Teaching students to locate and use these clues helps them learn to make educated guesses regarding the meaning of unfamiliar terms, which increases vocabulary and improves reading comprehension skills.

59. D: Vocabulary acquisition is a necessary component in the development of reading comprehension skills. When engaging with a new text, students may struggle to understand unfamiliar terms, impeding their ability to comprehend the text as a whole. Semantic mapping is an analysis strategy intended to help students develop word-learning skills by having them categorize the features of new vocabulary using a graphic organizer. This activity allows students to visualize the characteristics of and relationship between new words associated with a particular concept, thus strengthening overall understanding, and ultimately, reading comprehension. In this situation, having students complete a semantic map of words associated with the life cycle of plants would be beneficial in improving their comprehension of the informational text.

60. B: Reading comprehension refers to one's ability to read and understand a text. This skill can be categorized into three levels with increasing degrees of complexity. Literal reading comprehension refers to the ability to read and understand the basic meaning of words and sentences in a text. Inferential reading comprehension requires individuals to employ higher-order thinking skills by using contextual clues to determine what is implied by the author's use of literary techniques. Evaluative, or critical, reading comprehension occurs when readers connect a text to their own background knowledge and experiences to formulate personal thoughts and opinions on what they have read. In this situation, the teacher asks students to circle descriptive language that may indicate the motives of the main character. Students are tasked with using evidence from the text to support their thoughts and ideas about this topic, promoting the development of inferential reading comprehension skills.

61. B: Inventive spelling occurs when students employ their knowledge of letter-sound relationships to spell unfamiliar words. As spelling development occurs in stages, it is important to recognize that many young children will rely on inventive spelling as they begin learning to write. Encouraging this practice has students use their sense of phonemic awareness to sound out new words, ultimately improving their spelling abilities. However, the teacher must correct misspelled words to ensure proper development. Students that continue to use inventive spelling past the normal developmental stage may require additional support and intervention.

62. C: Helping young children understand that communication can occur in different ways, including both verbally and nonverbally, is an important component of developing their speaking and listening skills. Verbal communication refers to spoken language, volume, and intonation, whereas nonverbal communication includes such elements as eye contact, gestures, physical distance, and body language. Incorporating both forms of communication into the classroom for different purposes helps students learn to listen and respond appropriately in a variety of contexts. Further, this strategy supports students' oral language development, as accompanying verbal communication with nonverbal cues strengthens their understanding of its meaning.

63. D: Compound sentences occur when two independent clauses are joined by a conjunction, such as "and" or "but." This concept builds on students' knowledge of simple sentences, which consist of only one independent clause. Teaching the components and formation of compound sentences is important in developing students' ability to write on a more complex level, as well as their understanding of the characteristics and functions of the English language. Introducing compound sentences using kinesthetic materials, such as sentence-building strips, allows students to explore this concept in a hands-on learning setting. This strategy allows students to physically construct sentences using independent clauses and conjunctions, strengthening their understanding.

64. A: Effective writing includes a clear beginning, middle, and end. Teaching students this important skill is essential to developing their ability to write clearly and for a variety of purposes. As young children learn to express themselves in writing, particularly in narrative form, they may find it difficult to organize their thoughts in such a way. Story maps are a versatile form of graphic organizer that can be used as a prewriting activity to help students organize the events of their narrative pieces. This resource provides students with a visual aid to better arrange their ideas into a distinct beginning, middle, and end, improving the clarity and organization of their writing.

65. D: Distinguishing between syllable types is essential to developing the decoding skills necessary to facilitate reading comprehension, spelling, and writing abilities. Closed syllables are ones that include the short vowel sound followed by a consonant, whereas open syllables end with a long vowel sound. Students that struggle to recognize the difference will likely require additional support to ensure proper literacy development. Having these students practice forming words with letter tiles and reading them aloud provides a multisensory approach to develop this skill. This activity allows students to visualize, verbalize, and physically manipulate letters to strengthen their understanding of the different sounds produced by these two syllable types.

66. B: In language arts, sequencing refers to one's ability to recall and retell events of a text in the order in which they occurred. Teaching this important skill is essential to promoting success across content areas, as it contributes to the development of reading comprehension and writing, as well as the ability to understand and respond appropriately to directions. By kindergarten, students can reasonably be expected to retell the major events of a fictional work of literature in the order in which they occurred using visual aids as support. In this situation, having students sort events from the story using picture cards would most effectively promote their sequencing abilities.

Social Studies

67. C: Authentic summative assessments provide students with relevant and meaningful opportunities to demonstrate what they have learned. This assessment approach places learning in a familiar and real-world context, fostering students' personal connections for greater understanding. By second grade, students can reasonably be expected to create and use simple timelines to record events, including from their own lives. An autobiographical timeline project provides students with a personalized, engaging, and grade-level-appropriate learning opportunity to demonstrate their knowledge of how to sequence events chronologically.

68. B: Cross-curricular opportunities enrich instruction by demonstrating the relevance of learning in various contexts to strengthen students' understanding across content areas. When social studies is incorporated into other subject areas, students can explore its prevalence and application in daily life. In this situation, incorporating elements of social studies into a science unit on saltwater and freshwater bodies helps students understand the characteristics of different water resources, as well as how physical geography impacts human life. With exploratory activities such as a research project, students can learn how proximity to different bodies of water influenced human settlement patterns, and ultimately, other aspects of civilization, such as agriculture, diet, and commerce.

69. D: Young children learn best when provided with opportunities to actively participate in the process. For social studies instruction, such opportunities apply learning in real-world contexts, making it relevant and meaningful. In this situation, allowing students to vote on which review game to play promotes their understanding of the significance of voting as a civic duty to uphold democratic ideals and influence decisions related to the group as a whole. Further, in accompanying a unit on the election process with this activity, the teacher reinforces content-area material while developing students' sense of civic responsibility and their role in a democratic society.

70. A: Differentiating instruction is necessary to provide students of varying needs, abilities, skills, and preferences with equitable and engaging opportunities to participate in learning. Differentiated instruction takes several forms, and should occur throughout all stages of instruction. In this situation, the teacher plans to differentiate a lesson on a speech made by Franklin D. Roosevelt by implementing flexible grouping based on students' reading ability. Flexible grouping is the temporary grouping of students to accommodate specific learning needs in a given area. This strategy will allow the teacher to incorporate the appropriate scaffolds, such as chunking or modifying the text, to ensure all students have the supports necessary to learn effectively.

71. C: Teaching young children the notion of time, continuity, and change is necessary to develop their understanding of foundational concepts related to social studies, such as cause and effect, as well as how to accurately situate, recall, and make connections between historical events. Doing so should take place in a developmentally appropriate, familiar, and applicable context to ensure understanding. In this situation, labeling the days of the week as "yesterday," "today," and "tomorrow," as well has having students locate various events on a monthly calendar, shows how time functions in their daily lives. This strategy helps students begin to understand that time is linear and events happen chronologically, developing their sense of time, continuity, and change.

72. A: Providing young children with hands-on experiences to practice skills related to social studies strengthens their internalization of foundational concepts necessary for continued success in learning. Doing so helps establish a framework for reference that students can apply when learning increasingly complex topics in the content area. The ability to use cardinal directions, for example, is necessary for describing the locations of places and regions, as well as understanding more complex ideas related to geographic literacy, such as spatial awareness, latitude, longitude, and time zones. In this situation, having students use written directions to physically draw landmarks on a town map allows them to visualize cardinal directions in a hands-on, developmentally appropriate learning setting.

73. D: Incorporating digital resources into instruction creates an engaging learning experience in which students can interact with the curriculum in a meaningful way. In this situation, an online scavenger hunt on elements of Pennsylvania's history encourages a sense of inquiry, interest, and exploration about the subject. Such an activity increases the relevance of learning, as it lets students view and learn more about important buildings, monuments, and statues located in Pennsylvania in a realistic setting, thus strengthening their understanding of and connection to their community's history.

74. A: Understanding the concept of supply and demand—the notion that the availability of and desire for a product influences its price—is important for developing economic literacy. This skill is necessary for grasping increasingly complex topics, such as economic interdependence, price determination, and market competition. Students learn this foundational concept most effectively when provided with opportunities to interact with it in a relevant and meaningful way. By requiring more tickets for sought-after prizes, this teacher incorporates supply and demand into the classroom token economy in a real-world, applicable context to promote student understanding.

Arts and Humanities

75. A: Providing young children with a variety of artistic experiences is essential to promoting exploration, interest in the arts, and creative development. This includes teaching students to use a range of mediums, including paints, pencils, three-dimensional materials, and age-appropriate digital tools. While art materials should be accessible throughout the school day, it is also important to rotate which materials are available, to provide rich and varied experiences. Doing so provides exposure to multiple outlets for creative expression, allowing students to engage in the artistic process in a way that best suits their interests while promoting their ability to use a variety of materials when creating a work of art.

76. C: Teaching students to identify, describe, and apply basic elements of visual arts establishes the foundation for building artistic knowledge and creative development. Doing so helps students improve their own skills as they learn to manipulate these elements while fostering their ability to recognize, analyze, and interpret techniques in others' works of art. To design and implement effective learning experiences that incorporate the visual arts, early childhood educators must be familiar with the following basic elements:

- **Color**: the degree of hue, value, and intensity represented in the visual elements of a work of art
- **Line**: marks in a work of art that convey shape, movement, direction, and emotion
- **Shape**: two-dimensional objects in a work of art
- **Form**: three-dimensional shapes and objects in a work of art
- **Texture**: elements in a work of art that convey physical feeling

77. D: While formal evaluation of artistic ability is not typically advised in the early childhood classroom, conducting informal observational assessments attunes teachers to differences in students' learning styles, abilities, developmental levels, and needs. Feedback from such informal assessments allows teachers to adjust, modify, and implement supports to ensure all students can learn effectively. Doing so promotes positive learning experiences that encourage continued interest and exploration in the arts and humanities. By conducting an informal observational assessment, this teacher identified a student with a specific need, which means she can address it properly. In this situation, the student appears to have not yet developed the fine motor skills necessary to grasp certain artistic materials. Incorporating art materials of various sizes will provide the differentiation necessary to ensure that unstructured art time is aligned with this student's level of fine motor skill development, facilitating the student's full participation in learning.

78. B: Integrating the arts and humanities into other disciplines strengthens students' content knowledge while promoting creative development. Further, providing such cross-curricular learning activities illustrates the connection between the arts and other subject areas, increasing relevance by demonstrating their prevalence in everyday life. By having students apply their knowledge of acute, obtuse, and right angles to draw a realistic impression of a city, this teacher facilitates students' ability to make connections between art and mathematics. In doing so, this teacher fosters greater understanding of both disciplines by demonstrating how concepts learned in each content area can be applied to one another.

79. B: Incorporating music into daily learning experiences promotes development across domains, including students' ability to express themselves creatively. Further, incorporating group movement and dance activities into music instruction develops students' sense of spatial and kinesthetic awareness. Kinesthetic awareness is the understanding of how one's body moves, whereas spatial awareness is the awareness of one's body in relation to other individuals or objects. Through group movement and dance, students develop a greater understanding of how their bodies move, both individually and in relation to their environment, ultimately promoting the development of purposeful, coordinated movements. Providing students with physical props during these activities, such as hula hoops, ribbons, or sticks, enhances the development of these skills, as it encourages students to physically manipulate objects with purposeful awareness as they move within the group.

80. D: Incorporating opportunities for dramatic play into the early childhood classroom is essential to promoting students' ability to creatively express thoughts, ideas, and feelings as they make sense of the world around them. Through dramatic play, young children can imitate people, objects, animals, and scenarios observed in real-life experiences to organize, process, and develop a deeper understanding of their environment. After a lesson on the roles of firefighters, police officers, and emergency service workers, providing items for students to act out these roles in a dramatic play situation would reinforce their understanding.

81. D: Learning experiences in the arts and humanities should foster student inquiry and exploration. As students engage in the artistic process, they should be encouraged to take risks, test new ideas, and create new solutions to problems. Doing so promotes students' creative development and artistic ability while fostering continued interest in the arts. Asking students open-ended questions as they create works of arts promotes such exploration and inquiry. This strategy communicates genuine interest in students' artwork while instilling confidence to try new methods and explore potential outcomes. In this situation, asking the student what she thinks would happen if red and blue were mixed prompts her to try a new technique and build on her creative skills.

Mathematics

82. C: Before introducing a new concept in mathematics, it is important to determine whether students have developed a solid understanding of related fundamental concepts. Doing so ensures that students have the foundation of knowledge necessary to grasp increasingly complex concepts, problems, and methods. Administering diagnostic exams before a new unit of instruction gives teachers insight on students' level of background knowledge related to new material. The feedback provided from such assessments allows teachers to address areas of student need, clarify misconceptions, and identify any potential need for remediation to facilitate all students' ability to learn effectively. In this situation, students must have mastered the concept of place value in order to properly understand how to add and subtract numbers up to 1,000. This skill serves as an important framework for reference on how to set up addition and subtraction problems with two- and three-digit numbers, work within the appropriate columns, and regroup as necessary. Including this concept on a diagnostic test will help ensure students are fully prepared for success in learning when the new unit begins.

83. D: STEAM activities refer to those which simultaneously incorporate elements of science, technology, engineering, art, and math. Such multidisciplinary activities enrich learning by promoting higher-order skills such as critical thinking, problem-solving, and creativity while demonstrating the connection between content areas. For math instruction, STEAM activities highlight the prevalence of mathematical concepts in daily life, strengthening students' real-world connections to learning for greater understanding. In this activity, the teacher integrates all components of STEAM to provide a rich and multifaceted learning experience. Students will explore the properties of force and motion by creating a vehicle that can propel itself forward. Further, by using recycled materials to plan, design, and build the vehicle, students will employ concepts related to technology, engineering, and art. Math is involved because students will need problem-solving strategies to build a functional vehicle, and to calculate the amount of force required to propel it forward based on its weight.

84. A: Total participation techniques are whole-class activities in which students are prompted to actively participate in the learning experience. Such activities are intended to promote student engagement, strengthen understanding, and serve as a valuable formative assessment tool for teachers. By having students hold up their answers to multiplication problems on individual whiteboards, this teacher can quickly and formatively evaluate students' understanding. This strategy will provide the teacher with the feedback necessary to make adjustments throughout instruction, implement supports, and identify areas that may need reteaching to better meet students' learning needs.

85. D: Learning to keep track while counting is an important pre-numeracy skill that supports the ability to understand such concepts as ascending and descending order, cardinality, and one-to-one correspondence. When teaching prekindergarten children to count to ten, providing manipulatives such as counting chips creates an active, hands-on learning experience to support students in developing this skill. This strategy provides a kinesthetic element to learning by allowing students to physically move individual chips as they learn to count to ten, as well as a visual aid to help them keep track of how far they have counted.

86. C: Providing manipulatives for students to use as they engage in practice activities is an effective scaffold because it supports students as they develop the foundational skills necessary for grasping increasingly advanced concepts. Doing so aligns instruction to students' individual needs, skills, and abilities while promoting their learning and development in math. This strategy allows students to build understanding based on their current abilities and gradually develop greater independence as they work with increasingly complex problems.

87. A: Young children learn effectively when new mathematical concepts are placed in familiar, real-world contexts. This strategy fosters personal connections to learning, as students can see where it is relevant and applicable in their own lives. Showing images of analog clocks helps students internalize how to read them by providing a visual reference of how various times appear. Further, this concept is reinforced by corresponding each image to the time of each event on the class schedule. Doing so connects the idea of telling time with analog clocks to an immediately recognizable situation, making learning meaningful and promoting students' learning and development of this skill.

88. C: Learning to count money requires that students apply knowledge of several learned concepts, including addition and subtraction, skip counting, decimals, and the value of each denomination. Creating hands-on learning experiences supports students' ability to integrate these ideas when developing this new skill. By providing students with paper money and plastic coins as they work through this word problem, the teacher adds a visual and kinesthetic component to instruction that promotes students' understanding of how to count, add, and subtract money. This strategy will allow students to physically manipulate the various denominations of money as they work while providing a visual reference to keep track of their counting. Further, using representations of actual currency adds a realistic element to solving the problem, increasing relevance and strengthening students' personal connections to learning for greater success.

89. B: Number sense refers to a variety of early numeracy skills, including number recognition, counting, comparing numbers, and the ability to use mathematical language. Developing students' number sense is essential to establishing a foundation for understanding fundamental concepts in mathematics, so it must be emphasized in the early childhood classroom. Placing numbers in multiple contexts provides students with frequent and varied exposures to numbers throughout the school day. Doing so familiarizes students with numbers, how to use them, and what they can represent. By labeling the play area and students' desks with numerals, posting a number line in the classroom, and reviewing numbers with the whole class, this teacher demonstrates the prevalence of numbers in everyday life, promoting students' number sense.

90. C: Promoting students' ability to think algebraically in early elementary school establishes a foundation for thinking abstractly when working with increasingly advanced mathematical concepts. To achieve this, teachers should introduce math experiences gradually as students develop mastery. This method allows young children to progress through increasingly complex levels of algebraic thinking as they learn, while also demonstrating that the same expression can be presented in multiple ways. When introducing a new mathematical concept, teachers should begin by doing so concretely, then pictorially, and ultimately, in abstract terms. For example, in this situation, the teacher could begin by having students work with manipulatives as they solve addition problems, then present the equation using pictures of familiar objects, and eventually, show them only the numerical equation. Doing so helps students learn how to think algebraically when approaching new mathematical concepts.

91. D: The idea that fractions represent parts of a whole can be difficult for young children to grasp initially, as it requires a degree of abstract thinking. Incorporating manipulatives, such as pattern blocks, can help promote understanding for struggling students by adding a concrete element to learning. Pattern block sets are typically composed of squares, equilateral triangles, hexagons, rhombuses, and trapezoids, and are often used to demonstrate that shapes can be divided into equal parts. This resource allows students to visualize and physically manipulate shapes into equal parts, strengthening their understanding that fractions represent parts of a whole.

92. A: Understanding the concept of measurement is essential to developing skills across subject areas and in multiple real-world situations. Further, introducing measurement in early childhood establishes the foundation of understanding necessary for students to grasp increasingly complex topics, such as volume, height, weight, and mass. To introduce this idea, teachers should begin with the notion that some objects are larger or smaller than others, which prompts students to recognize differences in size. By asking students to arrange blocks from largest to smallest, this teacher encourages them to notice the size of each block and sort them accordingly, promoting early development of measurement skills.

93. B: Mathematical communication skills are the ability to speak and write effectively using mathematical terms. This includes using mathematical language to discuss one's thoughts, reasoning, and problem-solving strategies. Mathematical communication skills are necessary for developing and building on concept knowledge, as they promote students' understanding of their own thinking, connections between mathematical ideas, and ability to verbalize their processes. In this situation, asking students how they got a particular answer prompts them to consider their own reasoning and explain each step of their problem-solving strategy, promoting mathematical communication skills.

94. D: Teaching students strategies for estimation is beneficial in developing their mental computational skills, ability to make predictions, and understanding of reasonableness in terms of mathematical thinking. The ability to round numbers is an essential skill when working with estimation, as it allows students to simplify large numbers to quickly approximate an answer with a relative degree of accuracy. In this situation, students must be familiar with how to round numbers to the nearest ten and hundred in order to produce a valid estimation of the answer.

95. C: Teaching students to analyze and interpret data is essential in fostering their ability to identify patterns and relationships, compare information, and make informed predictions. This includes demonstrating that data results can be represented in multiple ways, such as bar graphs, pictographs, line plots, pie charts, or tally marks. Developing students' understanding of this concept is necessary to help them learn to analyze and interpret data in various formats, as well as determine when each one is most applicable. By having students create a bar graph based on tally marks to represent students' favorite seasons, this teacher demonstrates two ways that the same data can be presented.

96. B: Geometric awareness is the fundamental understanding of shapes, their characteristics, and their relationship to space. This includes recognizing the attributes of two- and three-dimensional shapes, differentiating between them, and describing their position and location in the environment. Teaching this skill in early childhood is essential to promoting students' spatial awareness, ability to grasp increasingly advanced mathematical concepts, and algebraic thinking and problem-solving skills. Encouraging young children to engage in geometric play, such as having them use blocks to build a tower, fosters an early sense of geometric awareness. Teachers can further enhance this development by asking students to create a drawing of their block tower before taking it down. Doing so prompts students to translate the physical form of their block tower into a drawing, promoting geometric awareness by encouraging them to focus on specific characteristics of each shape and their relationship to one another within the tower.

Science

97. A: Young children are naturally inclined to make observations about the world around them as they learn, process, organize, and test new ideas. Creating learning opportunities in which students are encouraged to do so promotes learning and development in science by fostering their inherent sense of curiosity, inquiry, and exploration. By selecting students each week to conduct a daily weather report and recording it on a class weather chart, this teacher prompts students to think scientifically about this concept by asking them to make observations about the natural environment to identify patterns and make predictions.

98. C: The ability to distinguish between fact and opinion is essential for learning and development across content areas, as well as in a variety of real-world contexts. For scientific learning, developing this skill helps instill the notion that science is rooted in fact, as well as the importance of seeking and producing verifiable evidence. Teaching students to distinguish between facts and opinions promotes their ability to support their own claims using valid data and determine the credibility of others' findings when engaging in scientific inquiry. In this situation, the teacher establishes the foundation for understanding the importance of verifiable evidence by first teaching students to distinguish between facts and opinions as they read through a text.

99. D: In science, a hypothesis is a testable prediction about the outcome of an experiment. These statements describe the intended effect of the independent variable on the dependent variable, and are the foundation of scientific investigations. Teaching young children to write an effective hypothesis is fundamental in developing their ability to follow the scientific method, so it must be taught explicitly. Giving students sentence frames to construct "if then" statements effectively introduces and develops this skill. Doing so guides students' writing to help them clearly express the cause-and-effect relationship between the variables in their experiment.

100. B: Integrating science into other disciplines strengthens students' understanding of learning across subject areas while highlighting the prevalence of scientific concepts in a variety of contexts. This makes science instruction relevant and meaningful to students as they begin to recognize situations in which their learning is applicable in daily life. In this situation, the teacher wants to highlight the relationship between scientific practices involved in agricultural systems, food production, and how it impacts the daily lives of people. By accompanying this science unit with a project in which students investigate the agricultural practices involved in making their favorite foods, the teacher creates an engaging, personalized learning opportunity that promotes understanding of the concept from both a scientific and social studies perspective. Through this activity, students can explore the interconnection between agricultural systems and the processes, individuals, and economics involved in producing their favorite foods.

101. B: Scaffolding science instruction helps to ensure that students of varying needs, skill levels, and abilities receive the support necessary to succeed in all stages of the learning process. Scaffolds can be implemented in a number of ways to accommodate a variety of learning situations. Many science activities incorporate hands-on, collaborative investigations, so strategic pairing scaffolds learning to facilitate all students' participation in the process. This strategy allows students who may need extra help to build upon the knowledge, skills, and understanding of their partners to promote their own learning and development in science.

102. D: Differentiating science instruction, particularly during project-based activities, is essential to fostering students' natural sense of curiosity and inquiry. Doing so aligns learning to students' varying interests, abilities, and skills to promote engagement and active participation. Science instruction should be differentiated throughout all stages of the learning process, including the assessment of content knowledge. By offering a choice in assessment using a project menu, this teacher can accommodate a range of needs in the classroom while ensuring all students are evaluated on the same criteria. This strategy would allow for flexibility in demonstration of understanding to promote learning and development in science for all students.

103. C: Introducing new concepts in science using active learning opportunities to promote exploration, creativity, and observation fosters students' natural sense of curiosity in the early childhood classroom. Doing so strengthens students' connections to learning by encouraging them to ask questions and test ideas, and helping them process new information. By having students create bird feeders to hang outside and observe, this teacher uses a hands-on learning approach to introduce the concept that animals have basic needs. This strategy will encourage students to watch as birds come to eat from the feeders they created, establishing a real-world foundation for understanding that living animals require food for survival.

104. A: Effective instructional planning in science is based on a set of central unifying themes within the field. This promotes student learning and development in science by establishing a foundation for understanding increasingly complex ideas while demonstrating the connections between scientific concepts. In this situation, students will learn that liquid takes the shape of its container by transferring water from a cup to a bowl, and then to a tray, thus developing a fundamental understanding of the law of conservation of matter. This law applies to the unifying concept of constancy and change; it states that although matter can change shape and form, its quantity remains constant.

105. C: Supporting students' learning and development in science includes helping them understand the purpose of scientific tools and when to use them. It is important to provide students with a variety of tools, materials, and equipment to promote active exploration and inquiry as they begin learning the steps of the scientific process. Doing so develops students' awareness that scientists use specific equipment to conduct investigations, gather information, and produce valid results. By giving each group a bin with various tools for conducting the experiment, this teacher encourages students to select which item will be most useful in gathering information, promoting their understanding of the purpose and uses of scientific equipment.

106. B: Introducing scientific concepts through developmentally appropriate practices is essential to establishing the foundation necessary for students to grasp increasingly complex ideas. Doing so promotes engagement and understanding by fostering students' natural sense of curiosity, exploration, and inquiry in a setting aligned with their interests and abilities. Young children internalize new scientific concepts most effectively when provided with active, relevant, and hands-on learning opportunities that foster personal connections to learning. This notion is strengthened by incorporating other disciplines, such as art, into science instruction. By first grade, most students can reasonably be expected to understand basic relationships between family members. Introducing the concept of genetics by having students create a family tree places learning in a personalized, project-based, and cross-curricular setting. This developmentally appropriate activity will ultimately strengthen students' understanding of genetics by allowing them to visualize similarities between their own family members, introducing the idea that individuals within the same family often share similar traits.

107. D: Placing new concepts in a relevant, meaningful context promotes scientific learning and development among young children. Doing so lets students recognize the real-world implications of their learning as it applies to their own lives, fostering personal connections for greater understanding. In this situation, placing labeled recycling bins in the classroom demonstrates to students how they can use concepts learned on the field trip in everyday situations. This strategy encourages students to incorporate recycling into their daily routines while simultaneously prompting them to classify recyclables by material to promote appropriate recycling practices.

108. A: Developing students' understanding of the causes of seasonal changes requires them to have a foundational awareness that the Earth revolves around the Sun on a tilted axis. This understanding helps students recognize that as the Earth revolves around the Sun over the course of a year, its axis points either toward or away from the Sun, causing varying degrees of sunlight. When learning about the causes of seasonal changes, young children may have difficulty comprehending how the Earth's position relative to the Sun affects the amount of sunlight they experience throughout the year. Young children build connections to learning through hands-on, project-based experiences, so having this student create a three-dimensional model of the Earth's revolution around the Sun would let the student investigate and gain clarification about this concept.

109. C: As young children begin learning about agricultural systems, food production, and its relationship to the environment, it is important that they also learn about the implications of the greenhouse effect. The greenhouse effect is a phenomenon in which certain gases in the atmosphere, including carbon dioxide, water vapor, methane, and nitrous oxide, trap heat and humidity. While an excess of these gases is harmful, the greenhouse effect is necessary for the growth of plants, so it can be beneficial for agriculture and food production. The greenhouse effect can be created by forming an enclosure in which plants can harness sunlight, but gases are not released into the atmosphere. This allows for plant growth throughout the year in a variety of climates and locations. Providing active, hands-on learning experiences is most effective in developing students' understanding of this concept in the early childhood classroom. By having students plant seeds and cover only some of them with a plastic bottle that has been cut in half, students can observe and compare how greenhouse gases affect plant growth. This will ultimately establish a foundation for understanding the relationship between the greenhouse effect and food production.

110. D: Scientific learning and development are best supported when young children are provided with opportunities that facilitate their natural inclination to observe and interact with the world around them. Such activities foster students' inherent sense of inquiry, as they are encouraged to use their physical senses to actively explore, investigate, and make discoveries as they build understanding of new concepts. In this situation, having students search for and identify different earth materials around the school campus would promote such inquiry by prompting students to physically interact with their immediate environment. In doing so, students would learn where these materials can be found in a natural setting, and would have the opportunity to observe, touch, and compare differences between them, thus strengthening their overall connection to learning.

111. A: During scientific exploration, asking students to record their thoughts and findings in a journal promotes inquiry and problem-solving skills. This strategy prompts students to reflect on their own thinking processes, work through problems, ask questions, and devise creative solutions. Further, having students keep observation journals can become a valuable formative assessment tool throughout instruction. By reading through these journals and providing feedback during the investigation, this teacher can gain insight into students' level of understanding, guide their process, and adjust instruction as necessary to support scientific learning and development.

Health

112. B: Gross motor skills refer to one's ability to engage in purposeful, coordinated large-muscle movements that incorporate the whole body, such as running, jumping, climbing, clapping, and stomping. These skills are essential to healthy physical development, so activities that incorporate such movements should be integrated throughout all areas of instruction in the early childhood classroom. By including a song in which students clap and stomp out syllables, and incorporating it into a language and literacy lesson on segmenting words, this teacher can strengthen students' understanding of the concept while promoting gross motor skill development.

113. C: Socioeconomic status may have significant implications on the quality of children's nutrition, physical health, and overall development. Families from low-income backgrounds often face several obstacles that may prevent access to resources and education related to adequate nutrition and health practices. This places children at greater risk for experiencing hindered development across domains, including cognitive delays, slowed physical growth, illness, and social, emotional, and behavioral issues. Further, as the foundation for nutrition, health, and fitness practices are often instilled in early childhood, those from socioeconomically disadvantaged backgrounds may be less likely to adopt healthy practices as they develop. If it is suspected that a student is in such a situation, it is important to refer the family to school- and community-based resources that can provide assistance.

114. B: The MyPlate website was created by the United States Department of Agriculture (USDA) to provide education and resources related to nutrition, health, and well-being at every stage of development. This visual and interactive website includes an array of information on the different food groups, portioning, and the nutritional benefits of consuming a variety of healthy foods. Having students explore the MyPlate website before beginning a meal-planning project would provide an active learning experience that establishes a framework for reference on how to make healthy food choices, as well as how these choices impact overall health and wellness. This would help students thoughtfully consider and make informed decisions about the foods they choose to include in their project.

115. D: An important component of health and wellness education is promoting students' understanding of how maintaining good hygiene helps to avoid illness. Instilling this concept in early childhood establishes a foundation for encouraging students to adopt good hygiene practices into their daily routines throughout life. Providing young children with active, hands-on experiences to teach the importance of hygiene demonstrates its relevance to increase students' understanding and connections to learning. In this activity, the glitter symbolizes germs. As students shake hands with one another, the glitter will transfer and stick to their hands, exemplifying how quickly illness-causing germs can spread. Further, as glitter is difficult to remove without proper handwashing, this activity shows how this basic hygiene routine helps avoid illness and maintain good health.

116. A: Modeling is a powerful instructional strategy in the early childhood classroom, as young children learn by imitating the actions, behaviors, and beliefs of adults in their immediate environment. Modeling a positive attitude and good practices related to health and physical fitness is essential to encouraging young children to adopt the same sentiment. Doing so helps to establish a foundation for students to engage in habits to maintain their own health, fitness, and well-being throughout their lives. In this situation, the teacher effectively models such a positive attitude by discussing her own exercise routines, incorporating movement into the classroom, and creating a learning environment that promotes health and physical fitness.

117. A: Teaching young children about healthy lifestyle choices and practices includes teaching them how to stay safe in the natural environment. This includes helping students learn to recognize and avoid environmental factors that can impact health and safety, such as harmful plants, animals, and insects. Using unplanned teachable moments strengthens students' understanding of this concept by placing it in an immediately applicable context. In this situation, the bees presented an environmental risk to students' physical safety. By telling them to avoid the bees and explaining that bee stings are harmful, this teacher effectively used this moment to provide students with a real-world example of how to identify potential dangers while outside in nature.

118. B: Promoting positive attitudes and confidence toward physical fitness and health requires that instruction, learning activities, and assessments are differentiated to align with students' individual needs. This includes providing students with a variety of options for physical activity. Doing so helps ensure that all students can participate in exercise and physical movement in a way that best suits their skill level, ability, and personal interests, encouraging their active participation. By providing multiple activity options at each station for students to demonstrate their strength, endurance, flexibility, and agility, this teacher can effectively differentiate the assessment to accommodate and engage all students.

119. D: Activities to develop students' fine motor skills are essential to helping them learn to perform a variety of daily tasks, including using tools with skill and control for specific purposes. When planning such activities, it is important to consider and align learning with students' developmental levels to promote engagement and confidence while providing the appropriate amount of challenge for skill building. By second grade, most students can reasonably be expected to possess a range of fine motor skills, and can begin engaging in increasingly complex tasks for greater development. Further, students in this age group learn most effectively through hands-on learning experiences in which they can physically manipulate learning materials. Introducing the concept of typing on a keyboard would provide these students with such an active learning opportunity while developing their dexterity and hand-eye coordination as they learn to correctly navigate a keyboard to type words.

120. A: While it is important to be aware of general expectations regarding gross motor skill development for each age group, early childhood educators must also understand that individual students will progress at different rates. When planning fitness instruction, recognizing these differences helps teachers implement the necessary supports, accommodations, and modifications to align learning with students' needs. Doing so promotes skill development while fostering students' confidence and positive attitudes toward physical activity. Diagnostic assessments are typically conducted prior to beginning a unit of instruction, and can be used to identify individual students' skill levels, abilities, and needs so as to differentiate learning accordingly. In this situation, performing a diagnostic skills test prior to beginning a unit on basketball will provide the teacher with insight into students' level of gross motor skill development so they can be placed in the appropriate groups.

121. C: Perceptual awareness skills are those which enable individuals to integrate sensory and physical motor skills in order to interact with the environment. This includes recognizing one's body and movements in relation to space, time, and direction. An example of a perceptual awareness skill is hand-eye coordination, which is the ability to use vision when performing activities that require controlled hand movements. This skill is essential for performing an array of daily tasks, engaging in physical activities, and learning to write. While hand-eye coordination is often acquired naturally as young children interact with the world around them, it is also important to provide multiple hands-on opportunities for developing this skill. Activities such as threading beads of various sizes allows students to practice using sight to guide their hands in purposeful movements, promoting the development of hand-eye coordination.

122. B: Teaching students to protect their physical safety by recognizing and responding appropriately to emergencies is an essential component of health and wellness education. This includes knowing the purpose of 911 calls in emergencies and how to make them. When teaching this concept, it is important to develop students' awareness of what constitutes an emergency to ensure they understand what to do in different situations. In following a visit by an emergency responder with a class discussion to differentiate emergency and non-emergency scenarios, this teacher can reinforce students' understanding of when it is appropriate to call 911.

123. C: Promoting healthy lifestyle choices among young children includes teaching them to identify and avoid unhealthy behaviors. Teachers must educate students about the negative impacts that drugs and alcohol have on overall health and well-being. Students must also be made aware that they will likely encounter instances in which harmful substances are present, and learn strategies for refusing them. In having students role-play scenarios in which they are offered drugs or alcohol, this teacher develops their ability to practice basic refusal skills by placing learning in a real-world context. As young children learn most effectively through play, so this activity provides a developmentally appropriate context for building strategies to avoid harmful substances and engage in healthy behaviors.

124. C: While individual children will acquire fine motor skills at varying rates, it is important to be aware of the characteristics, skills, and abilities associated with each developmental level. This understanding can help teachers implement age-appropriate activities to support fine motor skill development, as well as identify potential delays. By second grade, most students can reasonably be expected to grasp and manipulate small objects and tools for performing specific tasks. This includes independently engaging in self-help skills, such as tying shoes, zipping coats, and fastening buttons. Students who cannot perform these tasks independently by second grade may require further assessment of their fine motor skill development.

125. C: Non-locomotor skills are the ability to engage in gross (or large) movements of the body that are *not* used for propelling the body from place to place. Examples of such skills include bending, twisting, swaying, and stretching. Non-locomotor skills are an important component of overall physical fitness and health, as they contribute to building strength, balance, stamina, and flexibility. To promote development of these skills in the early childhood classroom, non-locomotor movements should be incorporated into daily learning experiences. By beginning each school day with yoga, this teacher prompts students to engage in a variety of stationary whole-body movements, supporting their development of non-locomotor skills.

126. D: Protecting students' health and safety requires that teachers follow specific precautions and guidelines related to physical activities. This includes making sure that all outdoor play equipment is clean, functional, and the appropriate size for students' developmental levels before allowing them to use it. Doing so is necessary to prevent injury and illness so as to provide them with a suitable, age-appropriate outdoor environment that promotes physical activity, learning, and motor skill development.

Practice Test #2

Child Development, Learning, and Assessment

1. Two prekindergarten students are playing alongside one another in the kitchen area of the classroom. While the students are talking to one another and sharing similar toys, each child is playing mostly independently. This is most characteristic of which of the following stages of play?

a. Solitary
b. Parallel
c. Associative
d. Cooperative

2. A first-grade teacher is planning a geometry unit on identifying and distinguishing 2D and 3D shapes. The unit will begin with a slideshow presentation to introduce the concept that includes writing information, visual representations, video clips, and a song to help students remember the characteristics of each shape. Throughout the unit, students will work together to construct shapes using a geoboard, participate in a class nature walk to identify geometric shapes in the environment, and apply their understanding by creating an original mosaic piece. By implementing these activities, this teacher demonstrates understanding of which of the following theories related to child development and learning?

a. Constructivism
b. Multiple intelligences
c. Social learning
d. Behaviorism

3. Which of the following would be indicative of atypical linguistic development for a prekindergarten student?

a. Mispronouncing multisyllabic words
b. Confusion when following multistep verbal instructions
c. Improper use of past, present, and future tense when speaking
d. Inability to speak in complete sentences using three or more words

4. To effectively design and deliver instruction that is responsive to all students' needs, teachers must recognize and understand the influence that which of the following factors has on learning and development?

a. The degree to which instruction aligns with state academic standards
b. Students' prior knowledge and experiences
c. Attitudes, behaviors, and values modeled by the teacher
d. Students' overall attitudes toward learning

5. During an unstructured play activity, a second-grade teacher notices two students disagreeing about whose turn it is to use a particular toy. Based upon the typical characteristics related to social and emotional development for students of this age group, the most appropriate response would be to do what?

a. Contact the students' families to inform them of the conflict.
b. Separate the students to avoid further disagreement.
c. Suggest that one student play with a different toy.
d. Allow the students to resolve the conflict among themselves.

6. A third-grade teacher is preparing an activity in which students will work together to construct a simple tower using recycled materials. Which of the following strategies would be most effective in promoting exploration and the development of problem-solving skills as students begin this activity?

a. Providing students with a variety of materials to choose from
b. Modeling the proper use and care of learning materials
c. Having students complete a KWL chart
d. Showing examples of previous students' work

7. To create a culturally inclusive learning environment that promotes acceptance and respect for student diversity, it is important that teachers do what?

a. Establish and maintain frequent communication with students' families.
b. Hold all students to the same high academic expectations.
c. Emphasize positive communication skills to promote healthy interpersonal relationships.
d. Teach lessons focused on holidays and traditions from different cultures around the world.

8. At the beginning of each unit of instruction, a fourth-grade teacher displays the state academic standards that students are expected to achieve on the chalkboard and reviews daily learning objectives each morning. Which of the following best describes the benefit of implementing this strategy?

a. Monitoring the pace of instruction to ensure all material is covered
b. Ensuring lesson activities are aligned with state learning standards
c. Reminding students of skills that will be assessed
d. Communicating the same academic expectations for all students

9. Upon enrolling in a new school, a third-grade student is given a screening test to evaluate her skills in reading, writing, and mathematics relative to other same-age students. This is an example of which of the following types of assessment?

a. Criterion-referenced
b. Norm-referenced
c. Diagnostic
d. Summative

10. A second-grade teacher works with a group of students that have varying skills, abilities, and needs, including individuals with learning disabilities and English language learners. During a math lesson on adding and subtracting three-digit numbers, the teacher groups students based upon ability level to work on a series of task cards that include solving word problems. Which of the following additional strategies would be beneficial in modifying instruction to support these students' learning and development?

a. Leveling the complexity of the task cards and incorporating visuals
b. Providing multiple examples of how to add and subtract three-digit numbers
c. Monitoring each group and checking frequently for understanding
d. Strategically grouping students with others that can provide scaffolding

11. A fourth-grade teacher has asked students to select a partner and score one another's most recent math quizzes. Which of the following is a potential limitation of utilizing such an assessment approach in this situation?

a. This method of assessment is time-consuming.
b. Individual learning needs are not considered during the scoring process.
c. Peer assessment lends itself to unreliability.
d. Only one correct answer is possible on math assessments.

12. Which of the following scenarios would be most effective in avoiding personal bias to ensure ethical assessment practices?

a. A team of third-grade teachers score the narrative essays of one another's students after deleting student names.
b. A second-grade teacher creates different versions of an end-of-unit assessment to protect academic integrity.
c. A fourth-grade teacher uses data from a diagnostic test to group students based upon ability for an upcoming language arts unit.
d. A first-grade teacher creates an alternative assessment to accommodate variances in students' learning styles.

13. At the beginning of the school year, a third-grade teacher asks students to complete an interest inventory. Which of the following is the likely intended purpose for implementing this strategy?

a. To build a positive classroom community through icebreaker activities
b. To communicate high academic expectations for the school year
c. To familiarize students with the teacher's instructional style
d. To gain understanding into students' strengths, needs, and preferred modes of learning

14. What is an important first step for forming a collaborative assessment partnership with students' families that can be developed and maintained throughout the school year?

a. Establishing a positive rapport with students' families
b. Self-educating about the needs and priorities of the community
c. Scheduling monthly family conferences for each student in advance
d. Creating a class syllabus to send home with students

15. A student in a fourth-grade class has been medically diagnosed with autism spectrum disorder and is especially sensitive to noise disruptions. According to this student's Individualized Education Program (IEP), the teacher must take measures to reduce distractions both during general instruction and in assessment situations. Based upon this information, which of the following accommodations would be most effective in providing this student with an equitable testing environment?

a. Allowing multiple and frequent breaks
b. Assistive technology, such as headphones
c. Providing an alternative testing location
d. Preferential seating at the front of the classroom

16. A second-grade teacher is preparing a science assessment on the elements of various aquatic habitats. One student in the class is identified as a developing ELL. According to the Pennsylvania English Language Proficiency Standards for English Language Learners PreK-12, which of the following linguistic supports would be most effective in facilitating this student's comprehension of the assessment content?

a. Assistive technology
b. Illustrations
c. A graphic organizer
d. Extra time for processing

17. A new first-grade teacher works with a culturally diverse group of students, including several ELLs. During a lesson, the teacher used a common idiom in English to explain a situation that many students did not understand. Which of the following best describes the reason for this?

a. Lack of context surrounding the idiom
b. Cross-cultural misunderstanding
c. Social language is more difficult to acquire than academic language.
d. Inadequate linguistic support during the lesson

18. A fourth-grade teacher is preparing to attend an annual IEP meeting for a student with a learning disability that impacts his reading comprehension and writing skills. To adequately provide information regarding this student's academic progress, the teacher should arrive to the meeting prepared with what?

a. Assessment data and samples of the student's work
b. A copy of grade-level state academic standards in language arts
c. A detailed outline of the curriculum
d. Additional learning resources that the student can use at home

19. Factors such as students' socioeconomic status, racial bias, and cultural misunderstanding are all possible causes of:

a. Lack of adequate learning materials and resources in the classroom
b. Overrepresentation of minority students in special education
c. Delayed qualification for IEPs among minority students
d. Poor student engagement and negative attitudes toward learning

20. In addition to building content knowledge, a kindergarten teacher wants to design instruction that promotes academic language acquisition among the ELLs in her classroom. Which of the following instructional approaches would be most effective in achieving this goal?

a. Scaffolding the linguistic complexity of instructional activities
b. Providing a print-rich environment
c. Implementing thematic units
d. Reviewing new vocabulary using flash cards

21. A second-grade teacher works with an English language learner with limited proficiency skills. In addition to creating a print-rich environment with authentic learning materials, this teacher often addresses the student using simple questions requiring one- or two-word answers and supplements instruction with visual aids whenever possible. By implementing these strategies, this teacher demonstrates knowledge of the characteristics related to which stage of second language acquisition?

a. Receptive
b. Early production
c. Speech emergence
d. Intermediate fluency

22. A fourth-grade teacher works with students that have a range of learning needs, including those with disabilities and English language learners. For a summative assessment on the life cycle of plants, this teacher allows students to choose from a project menu that includes a variety of activities. In doing so, this teacher demonstrates understanding of the strategies for applying what?

a. Universal design principles
b. Scaffolded instruction
c. Play-based learning opportunities
d. Culturally responsive teaching

Collaboration and Professionalism

23. A third-grade teacher scheduled a family conference to discuss concerns about a student's recent behavior in class and declining grades. At the conference, the student's mother disclosed that she has been especially stressed lately, and, as a result, her child has been increasingly defiant at home. This causes the mother to become frustrated, which ultimately leads to continued defiance from the child. According to the family systems theory, this is an example of:

a. Family projection
b. Emotional cutoff
c. Differentiation of self
d. Circular causality

24. A student's parents have been invited to attend a family conference to discuss their child's academic and behavioral progress, but they do not speak English. Which of the following does the school have the legal responsibility to provide in this situation?

a. The option to have the student translate for his or her parents
b. Translated written documents and a qualified interpreter upon the family's request
c. Samples of the student's recent classwork and assessments
d. A translated version of state and district academic standards

25. A second-grade teacher is participating in a regionwide professional development course focused on creating culturally responsive classrooms. For an upcoming assignment, the teacher plans to discuss his experiences working with ethnically diverse groups of students. Which of the following does this teacher have the legal and professional responsibility to do prior to submitting the assignment?

a. Take measures to protect the confidentiality of students' identities.
b. Ensure the assignment includes only factual accounts of his experiences.
c. Request permission from the school administration to disclose students' educational records.
d. Inform students' families of his intention to include them in the assignment.

26. To effectively serve as an advocate for students' needs, it is important that educators first take which of the following steps?

a. Establish positive relationships with students' families.
b. Strategize with colleagues about ways to improve the education program.
c. Communicate with students to learn about their needs.
d. Seek professional development opportunities focused on meeting students' diverse learning needs.

27. A fourth-grade teacher has noticed increasing tension recently among some students from different cultural backgrounds, and it has been negatively impacting the overall classroom climate. Which of the following conflict-resolution strategies could this teacher implement to reestablish and maintain a positive social context?

a. Contacting the students' families to address these concerns
b. Having students keep daily self-reflection journals
c. Holding a class discussion on the consequences of negative behaviors in the classroom
d. Leading regular restorative circles

28. A new first-grade teacher is preparing to attend back-to-school night. The community in which he teaches is diverse, and while he aims to establish positive relationships with students' families, he is uncertain of how to do so because he is unfamiliar with many of the cultural differences. Which of the following would be most effective in helping this teacher become more globally aware and practice culturally responsive communication?

a. Interacting with all families equally on back-to-school night
b. Self-educating regarding the beliefs, values, and traditions of students' families
c. Having students complete an interest inventory prior to back-to-school night
d. Scheduling individual conferences with students' families

29. The Individuals with Disabilities Education Act allocates additional funding for preschools to states with the purpose of supporting them in:

a. Providing resources for learning disabled children from socioeconomically disadvantaged communities
b. Identifying potential learning disabilities in children ages three through 21
c. Providing disabled children ages three through five with access to a free and appropriate public education
d. Developing and implementing IEPs for learning disabled students

30. A fourth-grade teacher has invited a student's parents in for a family conference to discuss the child's recent academic progress. The parents have previously had some negative experiences with the school system, and although they agreed to attend, they expressed some hesitation. Which of the following should this teacher do on the day of the conference to establish a positive rapport with this family?

a. Invite a member of the administration to also attend the conference.
b. Focus solely on discussing the student's progress in relation to state and district academic standards.
c. Provide the parents with printed copies of the student's grades and show samples of the student's recent work.
d. Create a welcoming atmosphere, begin with positive remarks about the student, and listen attentively to the parents.

31. A fourth-grade teacher is planning a science unit on animal habitats and would like to enhance student engagement by incorporating digital resources into instruction. Which of the following professionals in the building would be most helpful in assisting the teacher with this process?

a. The library and media specialist
b. The grade-level department chair
c. The curriculum coordinator
d. The reading resource teacher

32. A kindergarten teacher wants to improve their pedagogical skills in the classroom by learning more about recent developments related to ways in which unstructured play benefits cognitive development in young children. Which of the following resources would be most useful in finding this information?

a. An online discussion forum for early childhood educators
b. A recent article from an education-based website
c. A qualitative case study from an education research journal
d. A professional development workshop focused on strategies for integrating play into daily learning

33. Eliciting student feedback at the end of each unit is an effective method for engaging in:

a. Professional development
b. Self-assessment
c. Student-led learning
d. Educational research

34. A typically outgoing student in a fourth-grade class has recently been displaying withdrawn behavior and is reluctant to engage with his classmates. The teacher suspects that another group of peers may be bullying him. Which of the following does this teacher have the ethical responsibility to do in this situation?

a. Address the issue within the classroom and report his or her suspicions to the administration.
b. Continue to monitor interactions between these students to observe signs of bullying.
c. Speak with the involved students to determine the root cause of the bullying.
d. Suggest strategies that the student can use for positive conflict resolution.

35. For a research project on the history of Pennsylvania, a third-grade teacher has decided to allow students to use a digital app in which they can send direct messages to ask questions, discuss ideas, and respond to feedback related to the project. In accordance with Pennsylvania's Code of Professional Practice and Conduct for Educators, this teacher should do what?

a. Provide the school administrators with access to the app.
b. Ensure all interactions with students are professional in nature.
c. Save copies of online interactions with students for documentation.
d. Request parents' permission to use the app throughout the project.

36. Withdrawal, declining grades, sudden changes in behavior, and poor hygiene are all potential indicators of what?

a. Peer pressure in the classroom
b. A developmental delay or learning disability
c. A social or emotional disorder
d. Abuse or neglect in the home

Language and Literacy Development

37. A first-grade teacher is preparing a unit in which students will read a work of literary nonfiction. According to Pennsylvania's Academic Standards for English Language Arts for first grade, this teacher should focus the majority of instruction on strategies that support students in which of the following?

a. Proper book handling and developing print awareness
b. Constructing meaning from the text
c. Identifying grade-level high-frequency words
d. Group reading strategies that promote collaboration

38. According to Scarborough's reading rope, skilled reading is developed by a combination of factors related to:

a. Frequent exposure to literacy materials
b. Orthographic processing skills
c. Expressive and receptive language
d. Word recognition and language comprehension

39. Which of the following strategies for teaching new vocabulary best demonstrates knowledge of the Four-Part Processing Model for word recognition?

a. Reading new vocabulary words aloud and having students clap out syllables
b. Displaying sentence strips that include new vocabulary and corresponding images and reading them aloud to the class
c. Using sentence dictation exercises to develop students' receptive and expressive language skills
d. Having students create semantics features maps to learn new vocabulary and create word families

40. When introducing new high-frequency vocabulary, a first-grade teacher uses a mapping activity in which students separate, graph, and tap out the individual phonemes of each new word while reading them aloud. This strategy is likely intended to promote which of the following?

a. Automaticity
b. Prosody
c. Orthographic mapping
d. Receptive language skills

41. At the beginning of the school year, a third-grade teacher has students complete a simple interest inventory and then incorporates books into the class library based upon students' responses. Which of the following best describes the benefit of implementing this strategy?

a. Building a community of readers
b. Creating a print-rich environment
c. Promoting student-led learning
d. Differentiating literacy instruction

42. A kindergarten teacher has created four literacy learning stations in the classroom, with each focused on a specific component of phonics instruction. Every week, students are assigned to work in a particular station based upon their level of skill development, and the teacher monitors progress using an observation checklist to determine which stations to assign for the following week. Implementing this strategy allows this teacher to do which of the following?

a. Provide hands-on learning opportunities
b. Allow for flexibility and student choice
c. Differentiate literacy instruction
d. Modify learning activities

43. A prekindergarten teacher wants to incorporate online resources into literacy instruction to begin developing students' letter-sound correspondence skills. Which of the following digital activities would be most developmentally appropriate in achieving this?

a. An app in which students trace letters with their fingers while hearing them read aloud
b. Virtual flashcards that review each letter of the alphabet
c. A matching game in which students pair objects with the first letter of their name
d. A word-building activity in which students select the correct vowel to create CVC words

44. In a first-grade classroom, students are participating in a game in which they are assigned a vocabulary word written on an index card and asked to go around the room to find classmates with similar words. During this activity, the teacher walks around to observe and monitor student understanding. In this situation, the teacher is most likely using formative assessment to evaluate students' ability to do which of the following emergent literacy concepts?

a. Recognize CVC words in word families
b. Identify high-frequency sight words
c. Sort vocabulary words by category
d. Make word associations

45. While formatively assessing students' journal entries, a first-grade teacher notices that one student is having difficulty utilizing proper capitalization, spacing, and punctuation when writing. Which of the following intervention strategies would be most effective in supporting the development of this print concept?

a. Providing the student with a grammar reference sheet and having her rewrite the journal entry
b. Working with the student individually to help her practice correcting grammatical errors in sentences
c. Having the student complete daily sentence dictation exercises
d. Modeling different sentence structures and how to incorporate them into writing

46. A third-grade teacher has noticed that a student is having difficulty recognizing and spelling high-frequency sight words. In addition, when writing, he often skips words and writes letters backwards. Which of the following is the most appropriate response in this situation?

a. Provide the student with individualized instruction to develop his skills.
b. Pair the student with another that can provide scaffolding.
c. Implement response to intervention (RTI) services.
d. Refer the student for an initial evaluation with the special education department.

47. A prekindergarten teacher introduces a new tongue twister to the class each week. While reading the tongue twister aloud, the teacher emphasizes the first letter of each word and has students practice reciting it themselves. This strategy is likely intended to promote students' ability to identify and produce which of the following?

a. Rhyming
b. Alliteration
c. Consonant blends
d. Digraphs

48. A second-grade teacher is reviewing sight words with students. Included in the vocabulary list are the words "stitch," "witch," and "hitch." Each of these words contains which of the following?

a. An inflectional morpheme
b. A consonant trigraph
c. A vowel digraph
d. A diphthong

49. During a phonics assessment, a second-grade teacher has students individually read aloud from a list that includes both high-frequency and nonsense multisyllabic words. By including nonsense words on the list, the teacher is most likely evaluating which of the following skills?

a. Decoding and blending
b. Identifying rhyming and alliteration
c. Segmenting and substituting phonemes
d. Counting syllables

50. A second-grade teacher is preparing a unit on adding inflectional morphemes to words. Which phonics-related concept should this teacher review prior to beginning this unit?

a. Digraphs
b. Letter-sound correspondence
c. Long and short vowel sounds
d. Syllable segmentation

51. A fourth-grade teacher is planning to have students independently read a grade-level work of fictional literature. First, the teacher administers a diagnostic comprehension test and uses the results to select a small group of students that scored below grade level to work with the paraprofessional in the classroom. While in the group, students read independently, respond to discussion questions from the paraprofessional, and after reading, complete activities related to the text. This is an example of which of the following techniques for promoting reading comprehension?

a. Think-pair-share
b. Guided reading
c. Close reading
d. Contextual analysis

52. Prior to reading a new story aloud to the class, a kindergarten teacher leads students through a picture walk of the book. This strategy promotes students' overall comprehension by fostering their ability to do which of the following?

a. Make connections between illustrations and text
b. Identify the author and illustrator
c. Use proper book handling skills
d. Make inferences about events in the story

53. A first-grade student that is struggling to decode high-frequency CVC words likely needs intensive and explicit remediation in which of the following areas related to phonics instruction?

a. Differentiating open and closed vowel sounds
b. Phoneme substitution and deletion
c. Identifying beginning, medial, and ending phonemes
d. Letter-sound correspondence and blending

54. In the literacy corner of a prekindergarten classroom, a teacher has added pictures of familiar traffic signs, logos, and food labels. This strategy is likely intended to promote students' development of which of the following skills?

a. Decoding and encoding
b. Letter and number recognition
c. Letter-sound correspondence
d. Automaticity

55. A kindergarten teacher is reading a nursery rhyme aloud to the class. After each line, the teacher pauses and asks students to repeat it back using the same volume, intonation, rhythm, and pace. This is an example of which of the following strategies for developing prosodic reading skills?

a. Choral reading
b. Echo reading
c. Reader's theater
d. Syllable counting

56. A second-grade teacher is planning a unit in which students will write a short research essay on a land animal of their choosing. Which of the following activities would be most effective to have students complete at the beginning of this unit?

a. A KWL chart
b. A Venn diagram
c. A brainstorming web
d. A story map

57. A second-grade teacher is having students create vocabulary flip-books to practice adding prefixes and suffixes to root words. As students build each word, the teacher has them read it aloud to a table partner. This activity is likely intended to develop which of the following skills?

a. Letter-sound correspondence
b. Morphological awareness
c. Blending letter sounds
d. Phonemic awareness

58. A fourth-grade teacher wants to evaluate students' automaticity when reading aloud. Which of the following techniques would be most effective in assessing this skill?

a. Timing students as they individually read aloud from a grade-level text
b. Assigning corresponding comprehension questions to complete after reading
c. Having students circle high-frequency sight words in a vocabulary list
d. Asking students to orally recall major details from a reading passage

59. Students in a fourth-grade class have been assigned to read a short fictional novel over the course of several weeks. During the unit, the teacher plans to have students participate in literature circles. Which of the following best describes how this strategy is beneficial in promoting students' reading comprehension?

a. Students feel more accountable to read the book.
b. Reluctant readers can hear others read the text.
c. It provides an engaging and interactive context for reading.
d. Students' grades are dependent upon participation of all group members.

60. A first-grade teacher is planning to administer a diagnostic pretest before introducing a unit on the structure of simple sentences. Which of the following concepts should this teacher include in the test to ensure students' readiness for instruction?

a. Identifying basic nouns and verbs
b. Segmenting multisyllabic words
c. Recognizing conjunctions
d. Adding inflectional morphemes to words

61. Which of the following factors most strongly correlates with early childhood students' degree of success in building reading comprehension and writing skills?

a. Cultural background
b. Personal interest in reading
c. Oral language development
d. Socioeconomic status

62. When reading aloud to students, a second-grade teacher uses a different voice to represent each character's dialogue. This strategy is beneficial in promoting students' understanding of which literary device?

a. Personification
b. Point of view
c. Juxtaposition
d. Symbolism

63. To begin exposing students to informational texts, a prekindergarten teacher has incorporated a few simple printed recipes into the pretend kitchen area of the classroom. Which of the following questions would be most developmentally appropriate to ask students in this age group about one of the recipes so as to encourage them to interact with the text?

a. "Where can we find the ingredients for this recipe?"
b. "What would happen if we forgot an ingredient?"
c. "What are some similar recipes to this one?"
d. "What food does this recipe tell us how to make?"

64. When telling the teacher what he did over the weekend, a kindergarten student says, "I goed to the birthday party and eated some cake." How should the teacher respond in this situation?

a. Rephrasing the student's sentence by repeating it back properly
b. Ignoring the grammatical errors and responding to the student's statement
c. Asking the student follow-up questions to encourage discussion
d. Correcting the student's mistakes and asking them to repeat the sentence

65. Students in a fourth-grade class have been assigned to write a multi-paragraph opinion essay on whether school uniforms should be required. Which style of rubric would be most beneficial in allowing the teacher to evaluate students and provide them with feedback about their writing skills?

a. A holistic rubric
b. An analytic rubric
c. A single-point rubric
d. A developmental rubric

66. A fourth-grade class is reading a short fictional novel over the course of several days. As students read, the teacher prompts them to respond to a series of reflection questions regarding their reactions, thoughts, and opinions about the text using a reading response journal. This strategy is most likely intended to develop students' what?

a. Literal reading comprehension skills
b. Inferential reading comprehension skills
c. Evaluative reading comprehension skills
d. Problem-solving skills

Social Studies

67. A first-grade teacher has asked students to bring in a picture of something representing their heritage to create a classroom quilt. This activity is most likely intended to begin developing students' awareness of which main theme related to social studies learning?

a. Civic competence and democratic ideals
b. Awareness of one's own and others' cultures
c. Global connections
d. Individuals, groups, and institutions

68. In the art center of a second-grade classroom, a teacher overhears that a group of students all want to work on painting. However, there are not enough paintbrushes for each student in the group. This teachable moment can be utilized to develop students' understanding of:

a. Opportunity cost
b. Goods and services
c. Scarcity and choice
d. Incentives and choice

69. Which of the following strategies would be most effective in promoting students' sense of civic competence in a kindergarten classroom?

a. Assigning weekly classroom jobs
b. Modeling positive conflict resolution strategies
c. Reviewing the monthly calendar and having students identify important events
d. Incorporating clothing from other cultures into the dramatic play area

Refer to the following for question 70:

A first-grade teacher is planning a geography unit focused on how the weather impacts the way that people live. This unit will focus on how weather differs in the regions near the poles, the tropical regions, and the mid-latitudes.

70. Which of the following introductory activities would be most aligned with an inquiry-based approach for instruction?

a. Reviewing the four seasons and having students draw and label each one
b. Incorporating seasonal clothing into the dramatic play area of the classroom
c. Asking students to name activities they can do in each type of weather
d. Displaying pictures of clothing from various climates around the world and leading a class discussion about their similarities and differences

71. A prekindergarten teacher is planning instruction to introduce the concept of money. Which of the following activities would be most developmentally appropriate for children in this age group?

a. Asking students to create a budget for a pretend grocery shopping trip
b. Demonstrating how to add and subtract various denominations of money
c. Having students practice sorting coins by size
d. Inviting a bank teller into the classroom to discuss the purpose of financial institutions

72. Before students begin a research project on the founding of Pennsylvania, it would be beneficial for a third-grade teacher to assess:

a. Students' ability to differentiate primary and secondary sources
b. Students' knowledge of important buildings, statues, and monuments associated with Pennsylvania's history
c. Students' understanding of the purpose of a chronological timeline
d. Students' ability to identify different physical regions of Pennsylvania

73. A second-grade teacher is conducting a lesson on precipitation and would like to show students differences in rainfall levels across Pennsylvania. Which of the following instructional materials would be most effective in achieving this goal?

a. A political map
b. A topographical map
c. A thematic map
d. A physical map

74. In a third-grade classroom, students are participating in a scavenger hunt game in which they locate the country of origin of various classroom items. Such an activity is likely intended to begin developing students' initial understanding of which concept related to economics?

a. Scarcity and choice
b. Market competition
c. Foreign policy
d. International trade

Arts and Humanities

75. A fourth-grade teacher is having students replicate a drawing of a tree that has been flipped upside down. This strategy is effective for developing students' abilities related to the visual arts by promoting which of the following skills?

a. Spatial and kinesthetic awareness
b. Observation and attention to detail
c. Pattern recognition
d. Orthographic processing

76. After a social studies unit on goods and services, students in a second-grade classroom are working in groups to prepare an original skit in which they buy and sell items from a grocery store. Which of the following additional activities would be beneficial in encouraging students to use problem-solving skills to be resourceful?

a. Having students create their own props and costumes using recycled materials
b. Imposing a time limit for the length of students' skits
c. Assigning specific roles to students in each group
d. Providing each group with a rubric that outlines scoring criteria

77. Students in a third-grade class have been assigned to create a painting of a favorite family memory. After the project, the teacher plans to have students work with a partner to observe one another's paintings and write a short paper on similarities and differences between them. Such an activity is beneficial in developing students':

a. Recognition of basic elements related to the visual arts
b. Ability to give and receive constructive criticism
c. Awareness of and appreciation for diverse cultures and perspectives
d. Understanding of how to utilize various mediums for artistic expression

78. A kindergarten teacher wants to evaluate students' ability to recall key details from a literary text after reading a story aloud to the whole class. Which of the following strategies would be most effective in integrating the arts to achieve this goal?

a. Asking students to create a drawing of the main character
b. Having students work in small groups to act out the story
c. Assigning students to build a diorama of their favorite scene
d. Providing props and having students improvise a song about the story

79. An early childhood educator should demonstrate familiarity with which of the following basic terms related to dance?

a. Body, action, energy, time, and space
b. Rhythm, pitch, timbre, melody, and form
c. Spatial awareness, kinesthetic awareness, and perceptual awareness
d. Dexterity, agility, strength, coordination, and speed

80. A third-grade teacher is preparing a whole-class activity in which students will play a song using rhythm sticks. After conducting a diagnostic assessment, the teacher divides students into three groups and assigns each one to play a different version of the song. This strategy is likely intended to:

a. Demonstrate the basic elements of music
b. Allow for creative self-expression
c. Differentiate according to students' learning styles
d. Accommodate differences in ability

81. A kindergarten teacher asks students to clap out the rhythm as she leads them in singing a children's song. In addition to teaching the basic elements of music, this activity is beneficial in developing which of the following skills?

a. Phonological awareness
b. Hand-eye coordination
c. Orthographic processing
d. Expressive language

Mathematics

82. In order to grasp the concept of "counting on", it is important that students first develop a foundational understanding of which of the following?

a. Sequencing
b. Relative magnitude of numbers
c. Place value
d. Addition and subtraction

83. Which of the following questions would be most effective in developing kindergarten students' initial understanding of different tools' purpose and when to use them for measurement?

a. "What would we need to find out how cold it is outside today?"
b. "How tall are you?"
c. "Which book do you think is heavier?"
d. "How long does it take us to get from the classroom to the playground?"

84. In a third-grade classroom, students are working in pairs as they use a digital app to create an original musical rhythm using whole, half, quarter, and eighth notes. In addition to developing knowledge and skills in music, this activity is beneficial in supporting students' understanding of which of the following mathematical concepts?

a. Place value
b. Ordering
c. Fractions
d. Relative magnitude

85. During a math lesson, a prekindergarten teacher gives each student a small bag of candy and asks each to sort the candies by color. Then, the teacher asks students to count how many of each color were in the bag. This activity is likely intended to begin developing students' ability to do which of the following?

a. Describe the position of objects using ordinal number vocabulary
b. Identify and compare the attributes of shapes
c. Measure objects using nonstandard items
d. Represent, analyze, and interpret data

86. A second-grade teacher displays the following word problem on the projector screen and asks students to make guesses about potential answers:

John counts 30 trees in an orchard. There are 8 more apple trees than pear trees. How many apple and pear trees are in the orchard?

Then, the teacher checks students' possible answers on the board and records incorrect guesses on the following table:

Number of apple trees	Number of pear trees	Total number of trees

This table will be most beneficial in helping students utilize which of the following strategies to solve the problem?

a. Working backward
b. Eliminating possibilities
c. Guessing and checking
d. Using a formula

87. A prekindergarten teacher places five beads on a number mat and asks a student to count them aloud. After the student does so successfully, the teacher adds another bead to the set and asks her to count once more. The student proceeds to recount the entire set of beads beginning from one. Based upon this information, the student has not yet developed which of the following early numeracy skills?

a. Cardinality
b. Ordering
c. Number recognition
d. Rote counting

88. While informally observing students as they complete a worksheet on one-to-one correspondence, a kindergarten teacher notices that one student is repeating numbers as he counts. Which of the following instructional materials would be effective in strengthening the student's understanding of this concept?

a. A number line
b. Pattern blocks
c. Base-10 blocks
d. A counting mat

89. A kindergarten teacher could most effectively differentiate rote counting practice for students with varying abilities by implementing which of the following strategies?

a. Providing counting mats and manipulatives for students to represent different numbers
b. Creating number charts of varying lengths for students to practice rote counting
c. Pairing students with others that can provide scaffolding
d. Having students work in learning stations to practice rote counting

90. A second-grade teacher wants to begin developing students' foundational skills for solving multiplication problems. Which of the following strategies would be most effective in achieving this goal?

a. Reviewing steps for solving addition and subtraction problems of whole numbers within 100
b. Demonstrating how to split shapes into equal shares
c. Having students count unit cubes arranged in rectangular arrays
d. Providing students with a multiplication chart to use for reference

91. A third-grade student's continuous inability to do which of the following may indicate the potential need for further evaluation?

a. Multiply three-digit whole numbers
b. Compare and order fractions
c. Divide two-digit whole numbers
d. Add and subtract whole numbers within 100

92. A fourth-grade teacher is planning direct instruction for a unit on decimals and calculating simple percentages. Which of the following additional activities could this teacher implement to foster students' real-world connections to these concepts?

a. Creating a budget for a grocery shopping trip
b. Preparing and acting out a scene from a restaurant
c. Listing the ingredients from a favorite recipe
d. Solving word problems that include decimals and percentages

93. A prekindergarten teacher has recently incorporated Popsicle sticks into the classroom math center. This is most likely intended to begin developing students' foundational skills related to:

a. Creating shapes
b. Partitioning shapes
c. Sorting and classifying shapes
d. Comparing shapes

94. During a lesson on solving division problems, a third-grade teacher shows students how multiplication can be used to check the accuracy of their answers. In addition to developing students' skills in division, this strategy is beneficial in demonstrating which of the following?

a. Mathematical equations can be represented in multiple ways.
b. Applications of mathematical concepts in real-world contexts
c. Connections among mathematical ideas
d. The importance of developing mathematical communication skills

95. While teaching a lesson on telling time, a first-grade teacher uses phrases such as "half past" and "a quarter until" in addition to stating the numerical time. This strategy is beneficial in promoting students' development of which of the following skills?

a. Mathematical language
b. Reading both an analog and digital clock
c. Expressing problems in multiple ways
d. Skip counting

96. Students in a second-grade class have just completed an end-of-chapter test on basic multiplication facts. While scoring the assessments, the teacher noticed that many students did not perform well. Therefore, she is planning instruction to reteach foundational skills. Which of the following strategies would be helpful for this teacher to review to develop students' understanding of this concept?

a. Place value
b. Decomposing numbers
c. Counting on
d. Skip counting

Science

97. Students in a first-grade classroom are given photographs of various kinds of animals and are asked to sort them according to whether they have fur, scales, or feathers. As the students work, the teacher asks them why they think animals might have different types of body coverings. Asking such a question is beneficial in promoting students' development of which of the following?

a. Communication skills
b. Scientific process skills
c. Problem-solving skills
d. Scientific research skills

98. A second-grade teacher plans to use direct instruction to introduce a unit on the life cycle of plants. Which of the following additional strategies could this teacher implement to enrich the learning experience and strengthen student understanding?

a. Include examples of the life cycles of different kinds of plants in instruction.
b. Lead a class nature walk and ask students to describe the plants they observe.
c. Have students grow their own plants from a seed in the classroom.
d. Hold a class discussion about why some plants grow in specific regions.

99. A first-grade teacher is planning a unit on sunlight energy and wants to develop students' ability to make scientific observations. Which of the following strategies would be most effective in achieving this goal?

a. Showing a diagram that depicts the process of photosynthesis
b. Having students record daily weather patterns in a science journal
c. Creating a sundial to demonstrate the changing position of the Sun throughout the day
d. Asking students to notice where more plants are growing during a class nature walk

100. A kindergarten teacher places several toy animal figurines into the science area of the classroom and asks students to identify distinguishing features as they play, such as a duck's webbed feet, an elephant's trunk, or a bird's feathers. This strategy is most likely intended to use models for developing students' initial understanding of which of the following scientific concepts?

a. Heredity
b. Constancy and change
c. Adaptation
d. Land and aquatic habitats

101. A first-grade teacher wants to begin developing students' awareness of systems as a unifying scientific concept. Which of the following strategies would be most developmentally appropriate for children in this age group?

a. Displaying a scale model of the solar system in the classroom
b. Demonstrating that a toy car does not work if a wheel is removed
c. Having students build a block tower and knock it down
d. Showing examples of animal habitats in different regions of the world

102. A kindergarten teacher is planning a lesson on the states of matter in which she plans to demonstrate changes that occur to water at different temperatures. Which of the following questions would be most effective in prompting students to utilize scientific inquiry skills?

a. "What might happen if we leave this ice on the counter?"
b. "What happens to water when we freeze it?"
c. "Why do you think ice melts when it's hot outside?"
d. "How are water, ice, and steam the same?"

103. A third-grade teacher is conducting a unit on patterns that occur and recur in nature in which students observe and record weather patterns for a month. Which of the following additional activities could this teacher incorporate to differentiate instruction for gifted and talented students?

a. Pairing these students with others that need additional assistance
b. Having these students investigate local weather patterns throughout history
c. Asking these students to record weather data for an additional month
d. Assigning these students to write an informational essay about their findings

104. Students in a fourth-grade class are working in small groups to create an electromagnet and investigate ways to make it stronger or weaker. As they work, the teacher gives them red, yellow, and green color-coded cards that they can use to indicate their level of understanding. In addition to allowing the teacher to conduct formative assessments, this strategy is beneficial in promoting students' ability to do which of the following?

a. Indicate their level of engagement
b. Monitor their pace as they work
c. Determine the accuracy of their hypotheses
d. Self-assess their own progress

105. A prekindergarten teacher has incorporated soil, rocks, pebbles, and sand into the sensory bin in the classroom as students begin a unit on different geologic materials. Which of the following scientific learning tools could this teacher also include to best promote active exploration among students in this age group?

a. A microscope
b. A hand magnifier
c. A scale
d. A pair of tongs

106. To introduce a unit on the impact of litter on the environment, a kindergarten teacher leads the class in picking up trash from the school playground. Which of the following additional activities would be most effective in demonstrating this concept for students of this age group?

a. Placing the trash items into a bin of water for students to observe the effects
b. Having students sort recyclable versus nonrecyclable materials
c. Repurposing the trash items for an art activity
d. Discussing the difference between toxic and nontoxic materials

107. A second-grade teacher is planning a project in which students will design and construct a suitable habitat for a frog. Prior to beginning the project, the teacher should ensure students have a solid foundational understanding of which of the following concepts?

a. All living things are made up of matter.
b. Ecosystems are composed of several components that work together to function.
c. Living things require food, water, shelter, and space for survival.
d. Differences between the needs of plants and animals

108. Students in a first-grade class are participating in an activity in which they go outside and trace one another's shadows on the sidewalk in the morning, at lunchtime, and at the end of the school day. This investigation is most likely intended to develop students' fundamental understanding of which of the following concepts?

a. Living things require sunlight for survival.
b. Sunlight is a form of energy.
c. All planets rotate around the Sun.
d. Earth rotates on its axis every 24 hours.

109. A second-grade teacher is planning a unit on renewable versus nonrenewable energy sources. To best promote students' understanding of the difference between the two, it would be helpful for this teacher to first review which of the following?

a. The morphology of the words "renewable" and "nonrenewable"
b. Each form of energy and ways in which it is used
c. The process through which fossils are formed
d. Ways in which different living things use sunlight for energy

110. Students in a fourth-grade classroom have just finished writing conclusions for an investigation to determine which material was most effective for creating a functional parachute. In keeping with the steps of the scientific method, which of the following should the teacher have students do next?

a. Begin another scientific experiment
b. Repeat the experiment under the same conditions
c. Graph their data to compare with other students' findings
d. Adjust their procedure to determine whether it produces a different result

111. A third-grade teacher is preparing a unit on integrated pest management. To strengthen students' understanding of what constitutes a pest and why it must be controlled, this teacher should be sure to cover which of the following topics during instruction?

a. Common plants and animals found on farms
b. The difference between living and nonliving things
c. The habitats and survival needs of animals
d. Examples of ecological relationships found in nature

Health

112. A first-grade teacher has been conducting a unit on the importance of physical activity and making healthy food choices. In addition to classroom activities, which of the following strategies would be most helpful in reinforcing these concepts to promote positive attitudes toward health and fitness?

a. Providing students' families with information, resources, and suggestions related to health and fitness
b. Scheduling a class field trip to a fitness center
c. Having students track their food choices and daily activity using a digital app
d. Evaluating students' fitness levels using a criterion-referenced test

113. During a math lesson, a prekindergarten teacher has students use tongs to move and place counting chips as they create number sets up to 10. This strategy is likely intended to support students' development of which of the following fine motor skills?

a. Engaging in self-help skills with independence
b. Manipulating small objects using the pincer grasp
c. Utilizing tools with control and skill to manipulate objects
d. Choosing appropriate tools for specific tasks

114. Which of the following most significantly contributes to the growing problem of childhood obesity?

a. Cultural background
b. Socioeconomic status
c. Lifestyle factors
d. Genetic history

115. A second-grade teacher is planning a unit on nutrition and wants to focus on developing students' understanding of how food choices impact overall health. Which of the following strategies would be most effective in achieving this goal for students in this age group?

a. Having students sort pretend foods according to which part of the body they benefit most
b. Reviewing the MyPlate model for food portioning
c. Leading a class discussion on the function of major body systems
d. Asking students to log their food choices over the course of a week in a journal

116. Students in a first-grade classroom are working on a project in which they trace one another on large paper and label different body parts. This activity is most likely intended to begin developing students' understanding of which of the following concepts?

a. Ways in which the arts are prevalent across subject areas
b. The importance of physical activity and good nutrition
c. The location and function of body parts and major organs
d. How certain foods relate to specific parts of the body

117. Upon noticing that the class was beginning to lose focus during a science lesson, a third-grade teacher paused instruction to implement a brain break in which students stood up for a few minutes to stretch, run in place, and do jumping jacks at their seats. In addition to refocusing students' attention, this strategy is an effective method for doing which of the following?

a. Implementing cross-curricular instruction
b. Promoting fine motor skill development
c. Differentiating health and fitness instruction
d. Incorporating movement into daily learning experiences

118. During a language arts lesson, a kindergarten teacher is having students practice writing their names, addresses, and phone numbers. In addition to letter and number formation, this activity is beneficial in supporting students' development of which of the following skills?

a. Identifying harmful or dangerous situations
b. Emergency response preparedness
c. Gross motor movements
d. Orthographic and phonological processing

119. What is one of the first considerations that an early childhood educator should make prior to incorporating movement activities into the classroom?

a. The variety of available learning materials
b. Grade-level health and fitness standards
c. The physical arrangement of the classroom
d. Students' preferences and interests in relation to physical activity

120. While informally observing students' abilities during a class game of kickball, a second-grade teacher noticed that one student repeatedly failed to catch the ball in time when it was kicked in his direction. This may be indicative of a developmental delay related to which of the following perceptual awareness skills?

a. Body awareness
b. Spatial awareness
c. Directional awareness
d. Temporal awareness

121. At the beginning of the school year, a fourth-grade teacher had students complete a health inventory in which they answered several questions related to their daily habits, food choices, fitness levels, and interests regarding physical activities. This strategy was most likely implemented to help students do which of the following?

a. Identify environmental health risk factors
b. Recognize the importance of nutrition and exercise
c. Set personal health and fitness goals
d. Differentiate between healthy and unhealthy habits

122. During an outdoor play activity, a kindergarten teacher provides students with balls of several different sizes and weights as they practice throwing, catching, and kicking. In doing so, this teacher most likely intended to differentiate learning based upon students':

a. Fine motor skills
b. Gross motor skills
c. Non-locomotor skills
d. Perceptual awareness skills

123. A physical education teacher is planning an assessment for first-grade students to measure a variety of fitness skills. Which of the following activities would be most developmentally appropriate to include in this assessment for evaluating students' abilities related to balance?

a. Tossing a ball toward targets of varying sizes
b. Dribbling a soccer ball through a set of cones
c. Performing a variety of yoga poses that involve standing on one foot
d. Walking both forward and backward on a balance beam

124. The ability to dribble a soccer ball between cones, build a block tower, and trace an image on paper are all examples of which of the following?

a. Manipulative skills
b. Locomotor skills
c. Non-locomotor skills
d. Fine motor skills

125. A first-grade teacher is preparing a unit on nutrition for a group of students from ethnically diverse backgrounds. To promote inclusivity and positive attitudes toward health and wellness, this teacher should be sure to include which of the following into instruction?

a. Examples of both healthy and unhealthy foods
b. Information about the MyPlate model for food portioning
c. A variety of movement activities
d. Foods that reflect students' cultural backgrounds

126. Implementing group games such as tag, follow the leader, and hopscotch is beneficial in promoting the development of which of the following?

a. Locomotor skills
b. Non-locomotor skills
c. Manipulative movement skills
d. Object control skills

Answer Key and Explanations for Test #2

Child Development, Learning, and Assessment

1. C: Play serves an essential role for learning and development across domains. Through play, young children have the opportunity to gather and construct knowledge, organize information, and test ideas to build an understanding of the world around them. As children grow, they typically pass through six distinct stages of play. These stages, identified as unoccupied, solitary, onlooker, parallel, associative, and cooperative, are categorized by increasing degrees of social interaction and organized cooperation with others. Associative play occurs between ages three to four and is characterized by the beginning of intentional interaction with peers. During this stage, children may participate in the same activities, share the same toys, and communicate with or imitate one another, but the play is still largely unorganized and individual in its goals. In this situation, two children interacting with one another and sharing similar toys while still playing independently is most indicative of the associative play stage.

2. B: Howard Gardner proposed the theory of at least eight multiple intelligences to explain variations in how individuals think, learn, and process information. These intelligences are identified as logical-mathematical, visual-spatial, bodily-kinesthetic, verbal-linguistic, interpersonal, intrapersonal, musical, and naturalistic, with most individuals possessing dominance in one or two areas and varying degrees of strength in others. According to this theory, individuals internalize new information most effectively when it is presented through the lens of their dominant intelligence. Applying this theory as a framework for reference can help teachers recognize differences in learning styles, needs, skills, and abilities within their classroom. Doing so allows teachers to more effectively plan and differentiate instruction according to students' individual needs to maximize learning potential. In this situation, the teacher demonstrates understanding of Gardner's theory of multiple intelligences by incorporating multiple modalities for instruction into the unit to ensure learning is accessible, engaging, and comprehensible to all students.

3. D: While children develop and acquire skills at individual rates, there are typical developmental characteristics and progressions across domains associated with each age group. This knowledge can be used as a framework for reference when identifying typical and atypical patterns of development among young children. By prekindergarten, most children can reasonably be expected to understand and produce complete sentences using three or more words with accuracy and clarity. The inability to do so is indicative of atypical linguistic development relative to this age group. As language skills are essential to overall development, children that are not progressing at the same general rate as their same-age peers will likely require further evaluation to determine potential developmental delays or learning disabilities so that the necessary interventions and support can be provided.

4. B: All students will arrive in the classroom with varying experiences and levels of prior knowledge. Understanding that these factors will inevitably influence learning and development is essential to designing and delivering instruction that is responsive to all students' needs. By learning about individual backgrounds, strengths, skills, and interests, teachers can meet students where they are in terms of development while providing engaging, challenging, and relevant instruction that builds upon their abilities. Doing so creates meaningful and responsive learning experiences that align with students' individual needs and fosters personal connections for greater understanding.

5. D: Healthy social and emotional skills are developed through positive interactions with others and one's environment. As such, it is important to emphasize developmentally appropriate strategies for productive communication, self-regulation, and conflict resolution in the early childhood classroom. By second grade, most students with typical patterns related to social and emotional development are able to verbally resolve simple conflicts among themselves. Therefore, in this situation, the most appropriate response to noticing a disagreement between two students would be to allow them to work through it independently. Doing so promotes the development of problem-solving and communication skills and positive interpersonal relationships.

6. A: Providing young children with opportunities to engage in active exploration and problem-solving is essential to fostering healthy learning and development. Doing so prompts students to employ critical and higher-order thinking skills while eliciting their natural sense of curiosity and inquiry. Furthermore, active, hands-on learning opportunities that require the use of problem-solving skills are beneficial in enhancing students' connections to learning, thus promoting their ability to internalize new information. Providing students with a variety of materials to complete this activity forces them to employ problem-solving skills to consider, select, and test which items will be most effective in achieving the desired outcome of constructing a stable tower.

7. D: A culturally inclusive classroom is one that accurately and respectfully reflects the diversity of its students. Such an environment promotes positive self-identify as well as social and emotional skill development by encouraging students to value their own uniqueness while instilling acceptance and appreciation for others' differences. Teachers can create such an environment by incorporating lessons focused on holidays and traditions from different cultures around the world into the curriculum. Specifically, these lessons should reflect the cultures of the students within the classroom. Doing so would promote inclusivity by allowing students to see themselves reflected in daily learning experiences while providing the opportunity to learn more about their classmates' backgrounds and experiences.

8. D: Communicating the same high academic expectations for all students establishes a clear purpose for learning while fostering student motivation to create a productive and educationally focused environment. Doing so helps ensure that students clearly understand what they are expected to achieve as well as outlines short- and long-term academic goals for reaching learning targets. Furthermore, reviewing these expectations daily and connecting them to state academic standards places learning in a larger context to demonstrate the significance of each step within the overall process. This helps to make classroom learning more relevant and meaningful, thus increasing engagement and promoting active participation for greater academic achievement.

9. B: In education, norm-referenced assessments are those which measure students' performance in relation to one another. Whereas criterion-referenced exams evaluate students against a set of predetermined standards, norm-referenced tests compare students' scores relative to a group of same-age peers. Norm-referenced assessments can be used among a general student population or to compare individual progress within a particular group, such as those with learning disabilities or English language learners (ELLs). This method of evaluation is used for a variety of purposes in education, including screening individual students to determine levels of readiness for learning grade-level curriculum. Teachers can utilize the feedback from norm-referenced assessments to determine group placement, identify areas of individual need, and implement necessary supports and accommodations to ensure all students can learn effectively.

10. A: Adapting instructional practices, activities, and assessments to align with differences in individual ability and need is necessary to provide equitable and engaging learning opportunities that promote learning and development for all students. This includes modifying instruction as necessary for students that require additional support to make learning accessible as they build upon their skills and concept knowledge. In this situation, implementing flexible grouping strategies allows the teacher to differentiate the math lesson on adding and subtracting three-digit numbers according to students' ability level. The teacher could further support students, including ELLs and those with learning disabilities, by modifying the complexity of the task cards for each group and supplementing the word problems with visual aids. Doing so would be effective in scaffolding instruction to meet students' learning needs and providing clarification while implementing the appropriate amount of challenge for each group.

11. C: Peer assessment is a valuable tool in the early childhood classroom. This approach provides students with different perspectives while allowing them to build upon one another's skills and knowledge for continuous improvement. Further, peer assessment strategies are beneficial in developing students' ability to give and receive constructive feedback in a way that is positive, productive, and educationally focused. However, there are some instances in which utilizing peer evaluation as an assessment method poses limitations. For several reasons, such as student relations between one another, biases, lack of content knowledge, or uncertainty regarding the scoring process, students may inaccurately grade their classmates' work. Particularly in summative assessment situations, this produces unreliable results that teachers cannot utilize to accurately and objectively measure student progress, identify individual needs, or guide future instructional planning. As such, peer assessment is typically most beneficial and effective when applied in informal situations as students engage in the learning process to help build understanding.

12. A: To ensure ethical assessment practices, it is important that teachers take measures to maintain impartiality whenever possible. This includes avoiding any personal bias on the basis of race, culture, gender, skill level, or assumptions regarding individual students' abilities. Teachers must also recognize that unconscious bias may inadvertently influence the objectivity of student assessment and implement strategies to avoid it. Of the above-mentioned scenarios, switching class essays for scoring with grade-level colleagues while maintaining the confidentiality of student names would be most effective in avoiding such bias and maintaining ethical assessment practices. Doing so would help ensure that teachers are not acquainted with the students whose essays they are scoring, thus preserving objectivity and providing an accurate assessment of each student's progress.

13. D: Learning about students as unique individuals is an essential component to creating a positive, productive, and engaging environment. Understanding the diverse range of skills, abilities, and needs that exist within the same classroom allows teachers to differentiate and modify instruction in such a way that promotes learning and development for all students. Interest inventories refer to activities in which students are prompted to complete a variety of questions related to their personal strengths, interests, and learning styles. Implementing this activity at the beginning of the school year provides teachers with early insight into students' preferred modes of learning that can be used to guide instructional planning throughout the year.

14. A: Establishing a positive rapport with families early in the school year is an important first step for forming a successful, collaborative assessment partnership that promotes learning and development for all students. Doing so communicates the sentiment that family members are considered equal participants in their children's education, thus encouraging active involvement in the learning and assessment process. Further, families that feel welcomed and respected within the education program are more inclined to share information regarding their children's unique learning styles, needs, skills, abilities, and interests. This can provide teachers with valuable insight into how to develop the most effective assessment practices to meet students' individual learning needs and promote greater academic achievement.

15. C: The Individuals with Disabilities Education Act (IDEA) mandates that students with disabilities or other special learning needs receive the accommodations or modifications necessary to facilitate their full participation in learning, including assessments, to the same degree as their nondisabled peers. In this situation, the student may easily become distracted by noise disruptions in the general classroom setting during an assessment, thus interfering with his or her ability to effectively demonstrate learning. As such, providing the student with an alternative testing location that is free from distractions would be the most effective accommodation for providing an equitable testing environment.

16. B: The Pennsylvania English Language Proficiency Standards for English Language Learners PreK-12 serves as a framework for reference when planning content instruction and assessments. This resource provides educators with guidelines regarding expectations for ELLs at each stage of proficiency development as well as suggestions for linguistic supports to promote language acquisition while facilitating the achievement of academic standards. According to these standards, a student identified as a developing ELL is typically able to use context clues to determine the meaning of words and understand simple instructions that are accompanied by visual aids, such as illustrations. As such, supplementing the science assessment with illustrations would be most effective in providing context and clarification to support this student's overall comprehension and, therefore, his or her ability to demonstrate learning.

17. B: Cross-cultural misunderstandings occur when individuals from different cultures are unaware of one another's perception of both verbal and nonverbal forms of communication. Examples include the use of idioms, sarcasm, body language, proximity, and eye contact. When working with diverse students, particularly ELLs, it is important to recognize how cultural differences in communication styles, behavioral expectations, and classroom interactions affect teaching and learning. For example, the meaning of an idiom commonly used in American English will likely be unclear to students from other cultures that did not grow up speaking the language. Such an awareness will help to avoid cross-cultural misunderstandings and promote a culturally responsive learning environment.

18. A: One of the roles of the general educator in an IEP meeting is to provide updates regarding the student's mastery of grade-level curriculum standards. Teachers are expected to discuss the student's academic achievements as well as the effectiveness of current accommodations and modifications in facilitating his or her full participation in learning. Communicating this information is necessary for progress monitoring, setting academic goals, and determining the need for additional supports in the classroom. As such, it is important that teachers arrive to student IEP meetings prepared with documentation to reflect the student's performance and development, such as assessment data and samples of the student's recent work.

19. B: Minority students have historically been placed in special education programs at a disproportionate rate. Factors that may influence this include racial bias and cultural misunderstanding among educators as well as students' socioeconomic status. Racial bias or cultural misunderstanding may cause teachers to consider the behaviors, actions, and attitudes of minority students as indicative of a developmental disorder that requires special education services. Further, socioeconomically disadvantaged students often suffer lower academic achievement than their more affluent peers that sometimes gets attributed to a cognitive delay or learning disability when in reality it may be due to limited resources, lack of family involvement, and inadequate health and nutrition. Overrepresentation of minorities in special education programs poses significant academic, developmental, and social implications. Students unnecessarily placed in special education programs are unlikely to receive the proper support and resources for meeting their needs to facilitate growth and achievement. These students may also be held to lower academic standards and may experience limited opportunities upon graduation. Educators must recognize and work to eliminate personal bias and build culturally competent teaching practices. This includes developing an understanding of an individual student's needs, background, culture, and experiences through self-education as well as through professional development opportunities focused on working with diverse students.

20. C: When working with English language learners at all stages of proficiency development, it is important for teachers to recognize that the complexity and content-specific nature of academic language is often more difficult for these students to acquire. To promote retention, teachers should design learning experiences that demonstrate the use of new academic vocabulary in multiple contexts while allowing students several opportunities to practice interacting with the language. Thematic units are an effective strategy for promoting academic language acquisition in the early childhood classroom. This instructional approach implements activities across content areas that center upon a specific topic, thus providing multiple exposures to new academic vocabulary while simultaneously developing content knowledge. Further, thematic units often incorporate all areas of language development, thus promoting English acquisition across domains.

21. B: When working with ELLs, it is important for a teacher to understand the typical progression of second language acquisition to implement the appropriate supports for building fluency and promoting academic achievement. Second language learners pass through five stages of proficiency development, which are categorized as the receptive or silent phase, early production, speech emergence, intermediate fluency, and advanced fluency. During the early production stage, which lasts approximately six months, students begin building and producing simple vocabulary in the target language with the use of linguistic supports. Individuals in this stage have developed a vocabulary of about 1,000 words and can usually understand and respond to simple questions but continue to rely heavily on visual aids for clarification. By creating a print-rich environment, using visual supports to build vocabulary, and addressing students using simple questions that require one- or two-word answers, this teacher demonstrates understanding of the characteristics associated with the early production stage of language development.

22. A: Incorporating universal design principles into the classroom is beneficial in creating an engaging, equitable, and accessible learning environment that meets the needs of all students, including ELLs and those with disabilities. The universal design philosophy emphasizes the importance of differentiating instructional methods for engagement, representation, action, and expression of information. This includes allowing for flexibility in how students acquire, process, and demonstrate knowledge. In this situation, creating a project menu for a science assessment provides such flexibility by giving students multiple options to demonstrate understanding in a way that best suits their learning styles, preferences, and needs.

Collaboration and Professionalism

23. D: According to the family systems theory, the family exists as a singular, cohesive, and interdependent unit in which the dynamics are continuously shifting to achieve and maintain equilibrium. The interactions and behaviors of one family member directly influence the interactions and behaviors of others within the family unit. Further, the behavior of one family member may elicit a particular response from another that then perpetuates the original behavior. This reciprocity is referred to as circular causality and can be applied to identify the root cause of unwanted behaviors or negative relationships within the family unit. In this situation, the child's defiance is likely exacerbated by the mother's frustration, thus resulting in continued defiance and, ultimately, disequilibrium within the family unit.

24. B: The US Department of Education mandates that families with limited English proficiency skills receive all necessary linguistic accommodations and supports to facilitate their full participation in the education program. This includes translating all written documents into the family's preferred language, as well as providing translation services from a qualified interpreter. Doing so ensures that all families have equitable access to information regarding their children's education and can make informed decisions and contributions related to the overall learning process.

25. A: The Family Educational Rights and Privacy Act (FERPA) prohibits teachers from disclosing any information related to students' educational records without consent from the parents, authorized persons, or the individual student upon reaching the age of eighteen. This includes academic or behavioral records, medical history, and personally identifiable information, such as names, birthdates, or student identification numbers. As such, this teacher has the legal and professional responsibility to take measures for ensuring that information included in his assignment does not infringe upon his students' right to confidentiality prior to submitting it. While he may refer to his experiences working with ethnically diverse students in a general sense, he may not disclose any personal information that may reveal the students' identities.

26. C: Advocating for one's students helps to ensure that their needs are heard and then addressed by providing the resources and support necessary for their success in learning. Classroom teachers have the potential to serve as powerful student advocates. Doing so, however, requires that teachers work to build positive relationships with their students to become attuned to their individual needs. This includes creating a supportive classroom climate that facilitates and promotes communicating openly, asking questions, and practicing active listening. When students feel comfortable and encouraged to share ways in which their learning experiences could be improved, teachers can more effectively advocate for their needs.

27. D: The nature of the social context in the classroom poses significant problems for students' academic achievement, attitudes toward learning, and social and emotional development. Teachers must strive to create an environment in which all interactions, relationships, and behaviors are ones that help students feel safe, supported, and valued as they engage in learning. As conflicts will inevitably arise among students, this includes incorporating peaceful and productive conflict resolution techniques. Leading restorative circles is one such strategy that can be especially effective in achieving this goal. This practice, in which students gather either as a whole class or in small groups, provides a space for sharing ideas, discussing concerns, and working together to devise solutions through respectful and open communication. Regularly implementing restorative circles in the classroom helps students to build the empathy, self-responsibility, and active listening skills necessary to foster and maintain a positive classroom community and social context for learning.

28. B: Becoming globally aware requires that teachers recognize both the cultural differences that inevitably exist between themselves and students' families and the impact these differences have on attitudes toward children's learning and development. This understanding is necessary to practicing culturally responsive communication with families and establishing the foundation necessary for building and sustaining positive, collaborative relationships. Self-educating regarding the beliefs, values, and traditions of the people from the community in which one teaches is beneficial in providing insight into the community's needs and priorities for more effective communication. Further, engaging in this practice will help teachers gain understanding of norms surrounding appropriate verbal and nonverbal communication to ensure all interactions are respectful, accepting, and considerate of cultural differences.

29. C: The Individuals with Disabilities Education Act allocates federal funding to states for the purpose of supporting them in providing disabled students with access to a free and appropriate public education (FAPE) in the least restrictive environment. These funds are intended to equip schools with the staffing, professional development, resources, and services necessary to facilitate equitable learning opportunities for students with disabilities. Part B, Section 619 of this act allocates additional financial assistance for states providing special education services to prekindergarten children with disabilities between the ages of three and five.

30. D: The nature of the relationship between schools and families significantly impacts the quality of learning and academic achievement. Families that feel strongly connected to the school system are more inclined to share pertinent information regarding their children's learning styles, strengths, and preferences that teachers can apply to designing effective instruction. Regularly scheduled conferences throughout the year provide a valuable opportunity to build and sustain positive, collaborative relationships with students' families. In this setting, school staff and family members can discuss students' individual progress, address concerns, and share ideas related to the education program. For these meetings to be productive, it is important to first establish a positive rapport with the attending family members. Family conferences should be held in a comfortable, inviting environment to establish a positive tone that promotes open communication and should begin with positive remarks related to the students' strengths. Teachers and other attending school staff should ask relevant, open-ended questions that facilitate productive discussion, listen attentively, and respond appropriately. Doing so will help families, especially those that may be reluctant to engage with the school system, feel validated as equal participants in their children's learning, thus establishing the foundation necessary for building positive relationships.

31. A: Understanding the roles of each professional in the building is necessary to know whom to consult when planning instruction that promotes learning and development for all students. Collaboration with these professionals can help teachers develop effective strategies, approaches, and supports, as well as locate instructional resources and materials for meeting students' diverse learning needs. Library and media specialists are responsible for organizing, maintaining, and allocating all print and digital media resources in the school. In addition to educating students on how to navigate and utilize library materials, these individuals have knowledge and access to a variety of grade-level aligned media resources that can be incorporated into instruction to enhance the overall learning experience.

32. C: Education research journals are a valuable resource for staying current in the field of pedagogy and continuously improving one's teaching practices. These journals include articles and case studies containing recent and extensively researched information on specific topics related to pedagogical developments, theories, and practices. Teachers can utilize this information to develop their professional knowledge and skills in a particular area and implement new and effective strategies into the classroom for enhancing student learning.

33. B: Continuous self-assessment is essential to refining one's pedagogical skills and designing effective instruction that promotes learning and development for all students. Regularly engaging in this practice gives teachers insight into which strategies, activities, and assessments in the classroom were successful, as well as areas for improvement to further enhance the learning experience. Teachers can gain immediate and direct feedback for self-assessment by eliciting students' reactions and responses to instruction. This strategy provides teachers with deeper and more authentic information regarding students' overall engagement and understanding that can be used to adjust instructional practices as necessary to align with students' individual needs.

34. A: According to the National Association for the Education of Young Children (NAEYC), teachers have the ethical responsibility to ensure all students are able to learn in a safe, supportive, and healthy environment. Further, if a student is exposed to a situation that infringes upon his or her right to learn, teachers must take immediate and appropriate action to protect the child. Therefore, instances of bullying and harassment in the classroom must be addressed and resolved as soon as the teacher becomes aware of them. While anti-bullying and harassment laws differ between states, teachers are typically required to report suspicions of bullying to the school administration. The administration will then document the claims and initiate an investigation. It is also important that teachers directly respond to such situations in the classroom. This includes speaking with all involved students, working to resolve the issue among them, and reinforcing to the whole class the notion that instances of bullying and harassment are harmful and prevent others from learning.

35. B: Pennsylvania's Code of Professional Practice and Conduct for Educators outlines expectations for teacher behavior in relation to students, families, colleagues, and the profession. According to this document, teachers have the ethical obligation to maintain appropriate boundaries with students both inside and outside of the classroom. This extends to online spaces, as all electronic communication with students must be professional, including the nature of the subject matter, the extent and timing of the interactions, and the teacher's degree of openness. In this situation, the teacher would benefit from ensuring all interactions with students using the digital app are focused specifically on the research project so as to maintain appropriate and professional boundaries.

36. D: Protecting students' safety both within and outside of the classroom requires that educators are aware of how to recognize and address signs of child abuse or neglect. Children that are being abused or neglected in the home may display a sudden change in behavior in class. These students may become hostile, easily agitated, or disruptive. Other indicators include a decline in the students' grades, withdrawal, and poor hygiene practices. Upon observing these signs, it is important that teachers report their suspicions to child protective services immediately and follow the policies outlined in their district's professional code of conduct regarding procedures for reporting child abuse or neglect.

Language and Literacy Development

37. B: Pennsylvania's Academic Standards for English Language Arts outline performance indicators for students at each grade level and serve as a framework for reference when planning developmentally appropriate and challenging instruction. According to these standards, first-grade students should ultimately be able to construct meaning from a variety of fictional and nonfictional texts. As such, when planning this unit, the teacher should ensure that instructional strategies, lesson activities, and classroom assessments focus on supporting students in comprehension. This includes implementing activities before, during, and after reading, strategies for promoting vocabulary acquisition, and providing students multiple opportunities to demonstrate understanding.

38. D: The reading rope was created by Dr. Hollis Scarborough to demonstrate the intricacies of building fluent reading skills. According to this model, the ability to read is developed through an interdependent combination of factors related to language comprehension and word recognition. Language comprehension becomes strategic in nature over time and consists of the learner's background knowledge, vocabulary, literacy knowledge, verbal reasoning, and understanding of language structures. Word recognition becomes primarily automatic with proper development and refers to the learner's phonological awareness, decoding and spelling skills, and sight recognition. Both components must be developed through effective instructional practices in order to work together in building reading fluency. When planning language and literacy instruction, the reading rope can be utilized as a framework for reference to ensure all components necessary are incorporated for reading fluency development.

39. B: The Four-Part Processing Model for word recognition provides a framework for understanding how individuals acquire reading skills. According to this model, word recognition, and eventually, automaticity, occurs when four processors within the brain work together simultaneously. The phonological processor is responsible for differentiating, understanding, and attaching meaning to words and sounds in spoken language. Further, the orthographic processor works with the phonological processor to recognize and recall the meaning of written words as well as the sounds produced by written language. Through the context processor, individuals recall background knowledge and construct meaning using clues such as visual representations and surrounding words in a sentence. The meaning processor refers to one's knowledge of vocabulary, multiple meanings of words, and semantics. Helping young children become skilled readers requires that instruction incorporate all four components in the processing model. In this situation, displaying new vocabulary in a written sentence strip with corresponding images simultaneously stimulates the orthographic, context, and meaning processors. By reading the sentence aloud to the class, the teacher addresses the phonological processor, thus incorporating all components of the Four-Part Processing Model for word recognition.

40. C: Orthographic mapping refers to a process that occurs when the reader uses knowledge of letter-sound correspondence to recognize and recall the spelling, pronunciation, and meaning of written words. This process is necessary to build the word recognition skills and automaticity necessary for developing reading fluency. When introducing new vocabulary, teachers can stimulate orthographic mapping by having students separate the words into individual sounds to demonstrate the phonemic-graphemic relationship. This strategy helps students commit new words to memory, thus promoting vocabulary acquisition and sight word recognition. Further, having students tap out each phoneme as they read it aloud adds a kinesthetic element, thus strengthening connections for greater understanding.

41. A: Fostering a community of readers in the early childhood classroom establishes a foundation for literacy skill development and encourages lifelong reading. Regularly engaging in reading builds vocabulary by exposing students to a range of new words that may not be included in the general curriculum while promoting comprehension and fluency skills. Students are more inclined to develop positive attitudes toward reading when they have access to a variety of literacy materials that align with their personal interests. To build a community of readers, it is important that teachers make an effort to learn which subjects and genres their students find most relevant and engaging. Activities such as interest inventories are beneficial in providing this information, as teachers can utilize students' responses to create a classroom library that motivates students to read.

42. C: Effective literacy instruction is differentiated to align with students' diverse learning needs. By varying instructional approaches, learning activities, and assessments, teachers can meet students where they are in terms of development and build upon their knowledge for continuous growth. Incorporating learning stations into the classroom is a highly effective method for providing student-centered learning experiences because they allow teachers to implement multiple activities simultaneously to accommodate varying learning styles, abilities, and interests. For literacy instruction specifically, this versatile approach can be used to strengthen students' skills in a particular area. In this situation, the teacher differentiates literacy instruction by creating four stations related to phonics instruction and further individualizes learning by assigning stations based upon areas in which each student needs improvement.

43. A: Incorporating technology into literacy instruction can be highly beneficial in strengthening understanding of new concepts for emergent readers. However, when planning instruction, it is important to select digital resources that both align with state learning standards and students' level of cognitive development. Doing so ensures that learning experiences are accessible and engaging while providing the appropriate amount of challenge. Prekindergarten students are beginning to recognize letters and develop a sense of letter-sound correspondence. As children in this age group learn most effectively through hands-on, interactive experiences, a digital app in which students physically trace letters while hearing them read aloud would be most effective for promoting the development of these skills. Such an activity incorporates a kinesthetic element into learning, thus strengthening students' understanding of phonemic-graphemic relationships.

44. D: In the early childhood classroom, word association refers to the ability to recognize similarities between words and categorize them accordingly. Explicitly teaching this emergent literacy skill is essential to building reading fluency, as it promotes the development of receptive and expressive language, vocabulary acquisition, and comprehension. When introducing word association to young children, it is important to select developmentally appropriate activities and monitor students throughout instruction to evaluate overall understanding, identify areas of need, and make adjustments as necessary. In this situation, the teacher provides an active and engaging learning experience that allows students to interact with this concept in a hands-on, collaborative setting by implementing a word association game. Further, the teacher embeds formative assessment into the activity that can be used to guide future instructional planning by observing students as they participate.

45. B: As young children build emergent literacy skills, they begin to develop a greater understanding of increasingly complex concepts of print. For example, by first grade, most students are able to recognize and distinguish the features of a sentence, including proper capitalization, punctuation, and spacing. This knowledge is essential for reading and writing fluency, and as such, students that have difficulty with these concepts will require individualized support and additional practice. In this situation, having the student work to fix grammatical errors is beneficial in strengthening her understanding of how to identify and formulate a proper sentence. Further, working with her individually provides the additional support necessary for helping her improve her knowledge of print concepts to a grade-appropriate level.

46. D: While all children will acquire literacy skills at individual rates, there are general developmental characteristics associated with each age group. Recognizing atypical patterns of development is essential to identifying potential delays or learning disabilities so as to provide early intervention. By third grade, most neurotypical students have developed the ability to recognize and spell high-frequency sight words and write with a degree of accuracy and fluency. In this situation, the student is displaying possible signs of dyslexia, which is a learning disability that can significantly impede literacy skill development, particularly in the domains of reading and writing, if not properly addressed. As such, upon noticing these signs, it is important that the teacher refer this student for an initial evaluation to determine the need for special education services. Doing so will help to ensure he receives the supports and accommodations necessary to promote his literacy skill development.

47. B: Alliteration occurs when a group of words begin or end with the same letter sound. The ability to recognize and produce alliteration is an important phonological awareness skill that promotes students' ability to identify and begin segmenting individual sounds within words. Explicitly teaching this emergent literacy concept in the early childhood classroom establishes the foundation for developing letter-sound correspondence, correct spelling and word pronunciation, and ultimately, reading and writing fluency. Activities such as tongue twisters, songs, chants, and word games are beneficial in helping students notice when words begin and end the same, thus prompting them to begin recognizing and using alliteration.

48. B: As young children develop their language and literacy skills, teachers can begin introducing increasingly complex linguistic units into phonics instruction. A trigraph refers to a group of three letters that are pronounced as a single phoneme. Examples include the letter combinations "tch," "ear," "igh," and "eye." Trigraphs can consist exclusively of consonants, vowels, or a combination of both. In the above example, all three words are spelled with the "tch" letter combination to form a single phoneme; thus, all contain a consonant trigraph.

49. A: Nonsense words refer to those which are spelled and pronounced phonetically but carry no actual meaning in the English language. Incorporating these words into phonics instruction is a beneficial strategy for promoting and evaluating students' ability to decode and blend words with automaticity. Whereas students may sometimes be able to rely upon memory when reading aloud high-frequency sight words, nonsense words prompt students to notice and pronounce each letter sound individually. In doing so, students must distinguish individual phonemes and ultimately blend them together to correctly pronounce the nonsense word. When introducing nonsense words, teachers should begin with monosyllables and increase complexity to multisyllabic words as students develop their blending and decoding skills.

50. D: In the English language, inflectional morphemes refer to suffixes that change the grammatical tense, quantity, or possession of a word without altering the meaning of the root word itself. These linguistic units are bound to the root word and carry no semantic meaning on their own. Examples include "-ed," "-ing," "-s," and "-est." As this grammatical concept can prove especially difficult for young children to master, it is important that they have first acquired strong foundational knowledge related to a number of phonics-related skills. One such skill includes syllable segmentation, or the ability to distinguish the individual phonemes within words. Reviewing this concept prior to introducing inflectional morphemes would be beneficial in reinforcing students' knowledge of word structure and emphasizing the patterns of suffixes, thus promoting their ability to decode increasingly complex multisyllabic words.

51. B: Guided reading refers to a technique in which students work in a small group setting with the teacher, paraprofessional, or other educator to promote the development of reading comprehension and literacy skills. Students are typically grouped with others of the same or similar reading abilities and work closely with the educator to receive differentiated and individualized support when engaging with a text. While the specifics of implementing this strategy vary among groups and depend upon students' individual needs, guided reading groups typically follow a similar structure. Students begin by completing prereading activities to build background knowledge and provide context before reading the text independently. While reading, students respond to discussion questions prompted by the group facilitator and usually complete after-reading activities that are related to the text, building vocabulary, or specific concepts related to phonics instruction.

52. A: Familiarizing young children with the illustrations in a story prior to reading the text is highly beneficial in promoting overall comprehension. Doing so helps emergent readers formulate connections between pictures and corresponding text, thus promoting their ability to make predictions, sequence events, recall major details, and grasp the meaning of unfamiliar vocabulary. Activities such as picture walks, in which students are shown and prompted to discuss the illustrations in a story prior to hearing it read aloud, are an effective method for building students' background knowledge and providing context to establish the foundation necessary for greater overall comprehension.

53. D: CVC words are those that follow the consonant-vowel-consonant pattern, such as "hat," "put," and "big." These words are often the first to be introduced to emergent readers because they are typically familiar, spelled phonetically, and easy to pronounce. In order to begin recognizing and decoding CVC words, young children must first develop a sense of letter-sound correspondence and the ability to blend letter sounds for correct pronunciation. Students with weak phonics knowledge in this area will require intensive and explicit instruction to improve their skills to a developmentally appropriate level, as decoding CVC words is a foundational step for increasingly complex word recognition, and ultimately, reading fluency.

54. B: Environmental print refers to letters, numbers, and words that young children are regularly exposed to in their everyday lives, such as traffic signs, logos, and food labels. As students develop early literacy skills, incorporating environmental print into the classroom is highly beneficial in promoting letter and number recognition. Doing so provides familiar examples for identifying letters and numbers that have been taught, therefore strengthening students' connections by placing learning in a relevant and meaningful context. Allowing young children multiple opportunities to interact with environmental print helps build their understanding that written letters, numbers, and words convey meaning, thus establishing a foundation for developing emergent reading skills.

55. B: Echo reading refers to a strategy in which the teacher reads aloud a text and pauses periodically to have students repeat it back using the same level of expression. This method is used to build prosodic reading skills in the early childhood classroom, as the teacher models the appropriate pace, volume, timing, intonation, and rhythm when reading aloud to mirror that of spoken language. Developing students' ability to read prosodically is fundamental to fluency development because it strengthens their understanding of the connection between written and spoken language for increased comprehension and greater fluidity when reading aloud.

56. C: Introducing the fundamental steps of the research process in the early childhood classroom promotes writing skill development while establishing a foundation for success across content areas. This knowledge helps students understand how to answer their own questions and support their own claims by locating and thinking critically about relevant, credible evidence. Providing students with multiple opportunities to engage in research, particularly about topics related to their own interests, is beneficial in developing their understanding of the overall process. While students should begin by selecting a topic for research, this can sometimes prove overwhelming for young children. Having students complete brainstorming webs prior to beginning research can help reduce their overwhelming feelings and ultimately narrow their focus for improved writing. This activity allows students to think of questions, thoughts, and ideas related to a broad subject to help them specify their question or topic for research, thus helping them produce clear, coherent, and organized essays.

57. B: Students with strong morphological awareness skills are more effectively able to construct, comprehend, and communicate meaning when interacting with language; therefore, they experience greater development across literacy domains. Morphological awareness refers to one's ability to recognize and distinguish the individual morphemes, or units of language, that words are composed of. This knowledge promotes students' phonological and orthographic processing abilities, thus enhancing vocabulary acquisition as well as reading comprehension, writing, speaking, and listening skills. In this situation, the teacher is using a multisensory approach to build students' morphological awareness by having them create vocabulary flip-books to form words out of prefixes, roots, and suffixes. This activity allows students to physically interact with the words and practice using them by reading them aloud to a table partner, thus strengthening their connections and overall understanding of the concept.

58. A: Automaticity refers to one's ability to quickly and accurately recognize and comprehend the meaning of written words. This skill is foundational in the development of reading fluency; therefore, it should be practiced and assessed regularly in the early childhood classroom. Doing so is necessary to ensure students are reading at a grade-level appropriate pace, and it allows teachers to identify areas of individual need for additional support. Timing students as they individually read aloud from a grade-level text is an effective method for evaluating automaticity. This strategy allows teachers to determine how many words per minute the student is accurately able to identify and understand, thus providing measurable data specific to this area of reading fluency development.

59. C: The context in which reading occurs poses significant implications on students' overall interest and understanding. As such, it is important that teachers are responsive to students' needs to provide an environment that encourages reading and facilitates comprehension. While in some instances, a quiet area in the classroom dedicated to reading is ideal, young children also benefit from collaborative learning opportunities to build reading comprehension skills. Literature circles are a versatile strategy in which students meet with one another in small groups to discuss a text. During these meetings, students can either focus on an assigned text or talk about a book they are reading independently. In this student-led setting, each person is typically given a role related to a specific aspect of the text, thus promoting personal responsibility and ownership over learning for greater engagement. Implementing literature circles in the classroom allows students to verbalize and work through misunderstandings, questions, and thoughts about a text while building upon one another's knowledge in an interactive setting, thus promoting reading comprehension.

60. A: Simple sentences are independent clauses that are composed of a single subject and predicate. This sentence structure is typically the first to be introduced in the early childhood classroom once students have acquired a basic command of standard English conventions, which include parts of speech, spelling, grammar, and punctuation. It is important that teachers ensure students possess this foundational understanding prior because the ability to construct simple sentences is essential to writing fluency development. In order to recognize subjects and predicates, students must be able to identify basic nouns and verbs. Administering a diagnostic pretest to assess students' knowledge in this area prior to beginning a unit on simple sentences allows teachers to identify areas of misconception and provide clarification or reteaching as necessary. Students that are adequately prepared with the skills necessary to form simple sentences will be able to express themselves more clearly in writing and ultimately will develop a greater understanding of increasingly complex stylistic techniques.

61. C: Oral language development serves as a foundation for building early reading comprehension and writing skills; therefore, it is a significant indicator for achievement both in literacy and across content areas. Children with strong oral language skills begin literacy learning with a more expansive vocabulary, a greater understanding of the basic conventions of standard English, and the ability to express themselves more clearly. Encouraging the use of oral language in the early childhood classroom can be achieved by implementing multiple opportunities for children to speak and listen throughout the school day and across the curriculum. This includes reading aloud to students daily; incorporating rhymes, songs, and chants into instruction; facilitating discussion by asking open-ended questions; and promoting student interaction through purposeful play. Further, teachers can provide families with relevant resources, materials, and suggestions to reinforce oral language skill development at home. Doing so will help young children build a rich vocabulary and the skills necessary for successful reading comprehension and writing fluency development.

62. B: As young children develop reading comprehension skills, they can begin recognizing increasingly complex literary elements to construct greater meaning. Acknowledging different points of view that exist within the same fictional text increases students' overall understanding of the story structure and provides them with insight into the motivations, feelings, and actions of each character. This knowledge improves students' ability to think critically about a text because they can analyze the events that occur and evaluate their own opinions, thoughts, and judgements in response to each character. Using a distinct voice to represent the dialogue of each character is an effective strategy for introducing the notion that multiple perspectives may appear within the same story. Doing so helps students distinguish the individual personalities of each character, thus building their understanding of different points of view.

63. D: Exposure to a variety of informational texts in the early childhood classroom is beneficial in developing students' ability to construct meaning. Further, encouraging students to interact with these materials establishes the foundation for understanding how to identify the purpose and main idea of a text and locate supporting details. This can be achieved by incorporating familiar informational texts into daily learning experiences, such as including recipes in the pretend kitchen area of the classroom and asking relevant questions that prompt students to notice the text features. According to Pennsylvania's Academic Standards for English Language Arts, prekindergarten students can reasonably be expected to answer factual "who" and "what" questions about an informational text using features such as picture clues. As such, asking what a particular recipe is teaching students to make would be most developmentally appropriate in this situation for encouraging them to interact with the text.

64. A: Oral language development occurs when young children have multiple opportunities to engage in daily conversations. Doing so allows them to practice using spoken language while building skills as they listen to others. As students will inevitably make errors in grammar, word choice, and sentence structure, teachers must be diligent to reinforce correct usage while promoting students' confidence in speaking. When such errors occur, it is important that teachers refrain from explicitly correcting students, but rather, rephrase their sentence and repeat it back to model proper language use. This approach allows students to self-correct by listening and imitating the teacher's speech patterns for continuous skill development.

65. B: As students develop language and literacy skills, teachers can begin evaluating and providing feedback related to writing assignments with increasing specificity. According to Pennsylvania's Academic Standards for English Language Arts, fourth-grade students can be expected to demonstrate a degree of proficiency in terms of organization, clarity, grammar, word choice, and stylistic technique when composing multi-paragraph essays. For such complex assignments, using an analytic rubric is beneficial for examining and providing feedback regarding multiple components of students' work. Analytic rubrics break down criteria for scoring into several categories with detailed performance indicators in each one, thus outlining the characteristics of quality work to students while allowing teachers to provide specific and multifaceted feedback.

66. C: Reading comprehension refers to one's ability to read and construct meaning from a text. Young children typically develop through three increasingly advanced levels of reading comprehension ability as they build language and literacy skills. Beginning readers first comprehend text on a literal level and can understand the basic meaning of words and sentences. As students progress, they develop inferential reading skills, or the ability to interpret context clues to derive an implied meaning. Evaluative or critical reading comprehension skills occur when readers are able to relate what they have read to their own background knowledge and experiences to form personal thoughts and opinions. Implementing reading response journals into the early childhood classroom is an effective method for developing students' evaluative reading comprehension skills. This versatile resource can be differentiated to align with a variety of purposes and abilities as students are prompted to closely examine various aspects of a given text.

In this situation, the teacher asks students to reflect upon their reactions, opinions, and thoughts about the short novel, thus promoting the development of their evaluative reading comprehension skills.

Social Studies

67. B: Developing students' awareness of major themes related to social studies in the early childhood classroom requires that teachers implement activities to first demonstrate where these themes occur in daily life. Doing so places learning in a familiar, relevant context for young children and establishes the foundation necessary for applying these concepts to a larger scale. Cultural awareness refers to one's understanding of differences in beliefs, traditions, values, and experiences among individuals from other groups, and it is necessary for functioning as a productive member of society. Fostering this skill in the classroom promotes students' ability to communicate respectfully, collaborate with a diverse range of individuals, and build upon their own knowledge by learning to appreciate the perspectives of others. In this example activity, the teacher fosters students' ability to recognize that their background may differ from that of other individuals in the class, thus building a fundamental awareness of their own and others' cultures.

68. C: Harnessing teachable moments in daily classroom experiences is an effective method for placing major themes related to social studies in a real-world, immediately applicable context for greater understanding. Scarcity refers to instances in which the demand for a particular resource or service is greater than its availability. It often impacts the economic choices people make, or it may result in conflict. In this example, the teacher noticed that the demand for paintbrushes among the group of students outweighed the supply. This teachable moment could be utilized to begin discussing the concepts of scarcity and choice, the consequences of choices, and strategies for working together to devise a solution based upon the needs and wants of the group.

69. A: Teaching major themes related to social studies learning in alignment with students' developmental levels establishes the foundation necessary for understanding these concepts in a larger context. Before young children can grasp the implications of civil competence in terms of society as a whole, they must build knowledge of its meaning as it relates to their immediate environment. Civil competence broadly refers to one's understanding of societal and political structures and one's roles, rights, and responsibilities within them. At the kindergarten level, assigning weekly classroom jobs is an effective strategy for introducing the notion of civil competence. Doing so places this complex topic in a familiar context to help students build awareness of their roles as active participants in a group and develop their sense of personal responsibility to contribute meaningfully for the common good.

70. D: An inquiry-based approach to teaching social studies promotes young children's natural inclination for curiosity and exploration. Encouraging students to ask questions and make observations as they learn about the world around them establishes a foundation for understanding how major themes related to social studies apply to their daily lives and on a larger scale. Teachers can foster inquiry in the classroom by creating engaging learning opportunities that encourage students to devise their own questions and motivate them to seek the answers through active, hands-on investigation. In this situation, leading a discussion about similarities and differences between clothing from various climates leads students to question and want to learn why individuals in other parts of the world may dress the way they do, thus cultivating an inquiry-based learning experience.

71. C: Selecting appropriate teaching materials and activities for the early childhood classroom requires that teachers demonstrate awareness of the general characteristics and abilities relative to students' developmental levels. Doing so ensures that instructional practices are relevant, engaging, and accessible so as to best support learning and development in social studies. By prekindergarten, children are beginning to learn that money is used to make purchases, and they are typically able to sort items according to basic characteristics. As young children learn most effectively through hands-on experiences, having students practice sorting coins based upon size would be most appropriate in developing their initial understanding of the concept and purpose of money. Such an activity strengthens the students' connection to learning by allowing them to physically manipulate realistic instructional materials while building their awareness of different currency denominations.

72. A: As young children develop research skills, they can begin to demonstrate an increasingly advanced capacity for historical inquiry and analysis. According to the Pennsylvania Academic Standards for Social Studies, students should be able to identify and distinguish between primary and secondary sources by second grade. As such, third-grade teachers can reasonably expect students to incorporate them into a grade-level research project with a degree of accuracy and intention. Primary sources refer to firsthand accounts of historical events, such as photographs, interviews, or artifacts, while secondary sources are typically summaries, descriptions, interpretations, or analyses of historical events based upon information gathered from primary sources. Understanding this difference when engaging in historical research is integral to locating credible sources, discerning fact from opinion, and identifying multiple perspectives for greater understanding. Administering a diagnostic assessment focused on differentiating primary and secondary sources before beginning a research project would therefore be beneficial in this situation. This could be achieved through formal or informal techniques, such as a multiple-choice quiz, a sorting game, or a task card activity and would allow the teacher to identify areas of misconception to provide clarification and promote student success.

73. C: Recognizing and being able to interpret different types of maps is an important component of basic geographic literacy skill development. Exposing young children to and encouraging them to interact with various kinds of maps in the classroom is beneficial in helping them understand the function of each one and when each should be used. Thematic maps display information about a singular topic across a given geographic area, such as precipitation levels, temperature, or population, and are used to identify, analyze, and interpret patterns or trends across regions. In this example, a thematic map depicting rainfall levels across Pennsylvania would be most effective in demonstrating how precipitation levels vary in different regions throughout the state.

74. D: Integrating opportunities for purposeful play into the early childhood classroom is beneficial in supporting students' initial understanding of major themes related to social studies. Purposeful play allows young children to actively explore their immediate environment to discover the prevalence of these concepts in daily life, thus helping them internalize new information and ultimately apply it to a larger scale. In this example, a scavenger hunt game in which students search for the country of origin of various classroom items uses play to highlight the notion that many products used in everyday life come from other countries. Such an activity places learning into a familiar, real-world, and developmentally appropriate context to begin building students' fundamental understanding of international trade. Furthermore, implementing this game is an effective method for prompting further inquiry into the concept, such as why countries trade with one another, how products are transported, and the government's role in the process.

Arts and Humanities

75. B: Implementing strategies to develop students' sense of observation and attention to detail is beneficial in promoting their awareness and ability to apply knowledge of basic elements related to the visual arts, such as line, shape, form, color, and texture. This ultimately enhances students' capacity for creative self-expression as they learn to employ a variety of techniques when engaging in artistic endeavors. However, skill development in the realm of visual arts may become hindered by preconceived ideas of what objects should look like, as students may be inclined to refer to a mental image rather than the object itself. Flipping a drawing upside down and asking students to replicate it eliminates this mental image by prompting them to observe it from a different perspective. In doing so, students are more effectively able to notice details related to the artistic elements in the drawing and recreate them, thus developing their skills in the visual arts.

76. A: Incorporating the arts into daily learning experiences is beneficial in strengthening students' content knowledge while providing valuable opportunities to engage in creative problem-solving. Specifically, integrating creative drama into the classroom allows students to explore, test ideas, improvise, and devise solutions as they process, organize, and internalize new information. In this example, students will be required to employ problem-solving skills as they work through a variety of scenarios while creating their skit. Having students create their own props and costumes using recycled materials can add another layer of challenge to this project to further promote creative problem-solving. Doing so will prompt students to think critically about the limited available materials and make a series of decisions regarding how to best utilize them to create functional pieces for the skit.

77. C: Providing young children with opportunities to view one another's artwork is beneficial in developing their understanding of the notion that art and creativity vary among individuals. This concept is foundational in building students' awareness of and appreciation for diverse cultures and perspectives because it teaches them that ideas, thoughts, and feelings can be expressed in different ways without a singular correct answer. Having students observe one another's paintings and write about the similarities and differences is an effective method for exposing them to one another's artwork. Doing so provides them with the opportunity to notice intricacies in how their classmates' backgrounds and experiences influence their artistic expression and how their artistic expression may be similar or different to their own viewpoints, thus increasing their awareness of and appreciation for diverse perspectives.

78. B: Dramatic play is an integral part of early childhood learning and development across domains. In addition to promoting creative self-expression, dramatic play provides young children with the opportunity to explore, process, and internalize new information as it relates to the world around them. As such, teachers can utilize creative drama in the classroom as a method for evaluating students' knowledge and skill development in a variety of situations. Observing students as they engage in dramatic play allows teachers to gain insight into students' interpretations and overall understanding of new concepts and learning experiences. According to Pennsylvania's Academic Standards for English Language Arts, kindergarten students should be able to retell key details from a literary text in sequential order. By having students work in small groups to act out a story they heard read aloud, the teacher can assess this skill and clarify any misconceptions to promote comprehension and ultimately, language and literacy development.

79. A: Incorporating dance into the early childhood curriculum poses significant benefits across developmental domains. Through dance, young children gain a greater awareness and control of their bodies in relation to space, learn to cooperate with others, and build confidence through creative self-expression. Further, adding a kinesthetic element to instruction strengthens students' connections to learning for greater understanding. To design and implement effective instructional strategies, activities, and approaches for integrating dance into daily learning experiences, it is important that early childhood educators are familiar with the following basic terms:

- **Body:** this refers to the physical figure of the dancer. Dancers can utilize either the whole body or individual parts to create dance movements.
- **Action:** any physical movement of the body that occurs while dancing, including facial expressions
- **Energy:** how the dancer chooses to manipulate tension, force, flow, weight, and attack to convey meaning through movements
- **Time:** how the dancer moves through space in terms of rhythm, speed, tempo, and accent
- **Space:** how the dancer interacts with the surrounding environment, including in terms of direction, level, pathway, and relationships

80. D: In addition to teaching the fundamental elements, it is important that early music education promotes positive attitudes toward learning that encourage continued interest and exploration of the arts. This requires educators to recognize and accommodate differences in students' skill level, interest, and individual need when planning and implementing music activities. Differentiating music instruction allows teachers to meet students where they are in terms of development to provide engaging and appropriately challenging learning experiences that foster a sense of confidence while building skills. During whole-class activities, grouping students based upon ability is an effective method for providing such differentiation. In this example, the teacher likely conducted a diagnostic test to evaluate students' abilities in order to provide differentiated versions of the song's rhythm that varied in complexity. Doing so would allow the teacher to align the activity with differences in skill level to promote learning and development for all students.

81. A: In addition to fostering creative development, incorporating music and movement into daily learning experiences is beneficial in building students' knowledge and skills across content areas. Doing so integrates auditory and kinesthetic elements into instruction for a multisensory approach that strengthens students' connections to learning. Phonological awareness refers to the ability to identify, differentiate, and manipulate the sounds in spoken language. Having students clap out the rhythm of a song helps them to recognize differences among the sounds within it by prompting them to complete a physical movement to coincide with the words, thus developing phonological awareness skills.

Mathematics

82. B: Counting on refers to an addition strategy in which students count in ascending order beginning with the largest addend in a given equation. For example, if asked to solve the problem $7 + 4$, students must identify 7 as the larger addend and count upward 4 more until the sum of 11 is reached. This skill is beneficial in developing student's ability to quickly add numbers and recall basic addition facts. As the counting on strategy is most effective when students begin with the larger addend, it is important that they have first developed a foundational understanding of the relative magnitude of numbers. In elementary mathematics, relative magnitude refers to one's understanding of the quantity represented by a numeral. This helps students recognize number values and compare them and is therefore necessary for identifying the largest addend when counting on.

83. A: In the early childhood classroom, students begin learning that measurable attributes, such as length, width, height, weight, and temperature, can be quantified into data. Grasping this concept requires that students develop a foundational awareness of various measurement tools as well as an understanding of their purpose and when to utilize each one. To facilitate this, it is important that early childhood educators incorporate measurement vocabulary into daily learning experiences, provide a variety of measurement tools for exploration, and ask questions that encourage students to consider which measurement tool would be most effective in a given situation. In this example, asking students what they would need to determine how cold it is outside prompts them to think about which tool is most helpful in measuring temperature, thus developing their understanding that thermometers are used for this purpose.

84. C: Music instruction naturally lends itself to many opportunities for simultaneously supporting students' learning and development in mathematics. In early elementary specifically, music can be utilized to enhance students' knowledge related to counting, pattern recognition, time, and fractions. Harnessing these opportunities and using them to enrich daily classroom experiences is beneficial in strengthening students' understanding of both content areas while demonstrating the prevalence of mathematics in everyday life. By third grade, students are beginning to recognize simple fractions as numbers that represent parts of a whole. In this example, having students use a digital app to create an original rhythm requires them to work with wholes, halves, quarters, and eighths, thus supporting their understanding of fractions while developing their musical abilities and creative self-expression.

85. D: Developmentally appropriate learning experiences that foster an active, hands-on exploration of mathematics establishes the foundation necessary for building content knowledge and applying skills to increasingly complex topics. Providing early childhood students with the opportunity to physically touch, arrange, and visualize manipulatives, such as candies, while working with abstract mathematical ideas places learning in a concrete setting for greater understanding. In this situation, having students sort their candies according to color helps them conceptualize that measurable attributes can be quantified and represented as data. Further, asking students to count how many candies of each color were in the bag develops their fundamental ability to analyze and interpret numerical data representations.

86. C: In mathematics, guessing and checking refers to a strategy in which the learner makes educated guesses about the solution to a problem and checks for accuracy until the correct answer is achieved. This strategy is typically most useful in providing a starting point for approaching word problems in which some of the information has been given and the learner must calculate a missing number. Teaching the guess and check method in the early childhood classroom is beneficial in promoting the development of logical reasoning, critical thinking, and estimation skills, as students must apply what they know about a problem to devise reasonable possible solutions. The guess and check strategy is made more effective when students are provided with a table to utilize as a visual aid for recording incorrect guesses. Doing so helps students recall answers they have already tried and narrow down future guesses as they work closer to the solution.

87. A: Cardinality refers to the understanding that the last number counted indicates the total number of objects in a given set as well as the ability to recognize and attach a numeral to a set of objects. This early numeracy skill is integral for grasping a range of foundational mathematical concepts, such as quantity, numerical representation, adding, subtracting, and comparing numbers. Students that have developed a sense of cardinality can begin counting from the last number when additional objects are placed in a set. Students that recount the entire set from the beginning have not yet acquired this ability. Providing remediation in one-to-one correspondence and reinforcing this skill using manipulatives is beneficial in strengthening students' understanding of this concept.

88. D: One-to-one correspondence refers to students' ability to individually count items within a set with the understanding that each item can only be counted one time. Development of this early numeracy concept is essential to building a range of foundational mathematical skills; therefore it must be addressed explicitly when a student is experiencing difficulty. Formatively observing students as they work allows teachers to evaluate overall understanding and recognize when an individual is struggling so that they can implement the appropriate supports. Counting mats provide a multisensory approach to mathematical learning and can be differentiated to support students' understanding of a variety of skills, including one-to-one correspondence. Teachers can utilize this resource to have students physically move manipulatives as they count upward to represent a numerical value while simultaneously visualizing its quantity, thus strengthening their understanding of the concept.

89. B: Young children will inevitably begin school with a range of background knowledge and skills related to mathematics. For example, some students may enter school knowing how to count to 100, while others may only be able to count to 50. As such, it is important that early childhood educators differentiate instruction to meet students' individual needs while providing the appropriate amount of challenge for fostering skill development in mathematics. Rote counting refers to students' ability to recite numbers in sequential order and is necessary for building understanding of foundational mathematical concepts such as quantity, cardinality, addition, and subtraction. By creating number charts that vary in length for rote counting practice, students can develop this concept at a pace appropriate to their skill level. In doing so, teachers can meet students where they are in terms of ability to promote learning and development in mathematics.

90. C: As with all concepts in mathematics, multiplication skills build upon themselves. Implementing instructional strategies to develop students' foundational understanding of multiplication is therefore necessary to promoting success as they work with increasingly complex equations. Specifically, because multiplication requires abstract thinking processes, providing hands-on, concrete learning experiences is beneficial in building students' initial concept knowledge. Arrays are objects, numbers, symbols, or images that are situated in rows and columns, and they are highly effective in demonstrating the principles of multiplication. This tool provides a visual representation for solving multiplication problems, and by incorporating manipulatives, there is a kinesthetic element to strengthen students' connections to learning. Having students work with unit cubes arranged in rectangular arrays allows them to physically manipulate learning materials as they count, thus placing the concept of multiplication in a developmentally appropriate context to effectively build fundamental skills.

91. D: While individual students will progress mathematically at varying rates, it is important that teachers are aware of the general expectations for typical skill development associated with each grade level. This is necessary for teachers to identify areas of individual student need so that they can differentiate and incorporate appropriate supports into instruction as well as recognize the signs of a developmental delay or learning disability. By third grade, students should have acquired a degree of fluency in adding and subtracting whole numbers within 100. If a student is continuously struggling to do so despite the implementation of academic supports, it may indicate a learning disability or delay and would require further evaluation to determine the need for special education services.

92. B: As many mathematical concepts are abstract in nature, implementing concrete learning opportunities is beneficial in providing students with a real-world context to strengthen understanding. Doing so demonstrates the applications of math in everyday life, thus helping students build personal connections to learning that make the overall experience more relevant and meaningful. An assignment in which students prepare and act out a skit from a restaurant requires them to apply knowledge of decimals when selecting items from the menu and calculating their bill and use percentages when determining the tax and tip. Such an activity illustrates the real-world applications of these concepts by placing them in a familiar setting. Further, incorporating dramatic play into math instruction allows young students to process, organize, and ultimately internalize new information for greater retention.

93. A: Young children develop foundational mathematical skills through active, hands-on learning opportunities that foster their natural sense of exploration and curiosity. Incorporating manipulatives into instruction is beneficial in facilitating such exploration and providing concrete experiences for building knowledge about abstract mathematical concepts. A variety of simple items can be utilized as manipulatives for mathematics instruction. Popsicle sticks, for example, are an effective learning tool for promoting students' fundamental skills in creating two-dimensional shapes. Working with Popsicle sticks for this purpose allows students to physically touch and experiment with learning materials as they begin to develop an understanding of the attributes of different shapes and how to compose them.

94. C: Demonstrating the connection among mathematical ideas is beneficial in increasing relevancy and understanding for young children by establishing a clear purpose for learning. In doing so, students develop an awareness that mathematical skills build upon one another, and they learn how to apply previously learned knowledge to increasingly complex concepts. Further, teaching students to recognize these connections promotes continuous mathematical skill development by providing students with a variety of strategies to utilize when approaching new topics. While early childhood students may initially view multiplication and division as opposites of one another, demonstrating that the two are interrelated strengthens students' understanding of both operations. By showing students that multiplication can be used to check for accuracy when solving division problems, this teacher illustrates the inverse relationship between the two concepts, thus reinforcing the notion that many mathematical ideas are connected.

95. A: Emphasizing the use and acquisition of mathematical language skills in the early childhood classroom is essential to strengthening content knowledge and building a foundation for understanding increasingly complex topics. Students with strong mathematical language skills are more effectively able to understand and verbalize their thinking processes, work through problem-solving strategies, and make connections between mathematical ideas. An important component in developing students' ability to use mathematical language includes demonstrating that many concepts can be communicated in a variety of ways. By incorporating common phrases associated with telling time in addition to stating the time numerically, this teacher builds students' mathematical vocabulary. In addition, incorporating the phrases "half past" and "a quarter until" specifically is beneficial in fostering students' connections between time and fractions.

96. D: Summative assessments are administered at the end of an instructional unit to evaluate students' mastery of learning objectives. In mathematics instruction, these assessments provide teachers with feedback regarding areas of individual or whole-class need to plan future instruction and determine the need for reteaching specific skills. In this situation, the fact that many students in the class did not perform well on a summative assessment focused on basic multiplication facts indicates the need for whole-class reteaching of foundational skills. One such skill that would be beneficial to review includes skip counting. Skip counting refers to a strategy for counting in ascending order in specific intervals, such as by twos, fives, or tens. Reteaching this concept promotes students' ability to quickly count equal sets of numbers, thus establishing the foundation of understanding necessary to solve basic multiplication problems.

Science

97. B: Asking open-ended questions as students engage in learning fosters their natural sense of curiosity to promote the development of scientific process skills. These skills refer to students' ability to observe, classify and sort, measure, make inferences and predictions, and communicate findings, and they are foundational for continuous scientific learning and development. In this situation, students must engage in the scientific process as they sort and classify pictures of animals according to whether they have fur, scales, or feathers. The teacher further promotes the development of these skills by asking students to consider why animals might have different body coverings. Such an open-ended question encourages students to verbalize their thinking and make observations that will lead to further inquiry and exploration.

98. C: Early childhood educators facilitate scientific learning and development by providing learning experiences that promote active exploration of the natural world. Doing so allows students to observe, experiment with, and process new information as it applies to their immediate environment, thus enriching instruction and fostering a greater understanding of scientific concepts. In this situation, the teacher can enhance a unit on the plant life cycle by implementing a project in which students grow their own plants from seeds. Such an activity would bring materials from the natural world into the classroom for hands-on exploration and would strengthen students' connections to learning by placing it in a relevant context as they observe each stage of the plant life cycle in real time.

99. D: Scientific learning and development occur naturally when early childhood educators facilitate learning experiences that harness students' inherent sense of curiosity. Such opportunities foster students' natural inclination to make observations that elicit further inquiry as they organize, process, experiment with, and interpret the world around them. In this example, asking students to observe differences in plant growth during a class nature walk encourages them to think scientifically and notice that more plants tend to grow in sunlit areas than in shaded ones. This can be utilized to introduce the notion that plants depend on sunlight for energy to grow as well as prompt further investigation to build scientific knowledge and understanding.

100. C: Placing scientific concepts in a developmentally appropriate context for learning is necessary to build students' fundamental concept knowledge and promote understanding when approaching increasingly complex ideas. At the kindergarten level, teachers can expect students to be able to identify distinguishing features among various types of animals, such as a duck's webbed feet, a bird's feathers, or an elephant's trunk. As young children learn most effectively through play and exploration, placing lifelike models of animals into the science area allows them to actively engage with learning materials and observe differences in the animals' physical characteristics. By asking students to identify these distinguishing features as they play, this teacher prompts further inquiry and establishes the foundation for developing their initial understanding that animals physically adapt to survive in different habitats.

101. B: Presenting complex unifying themes of science through age-appropriate strategies strengthens students' understanding as they continuously build scientific knowledge and skills. When instructional practices align with students' developmental capabilities, learning becomes relevant, meaningful, and accessible for them as they begin to recognize where major concepts are applicable in daily life. In science, the unifying concept of systems refers to the notion that all things are composed of interconnected parts that must work together simultaneously to function. Demonstrating that a toy car does not work if a wheel is removed simplifies this idea in a way that first-grade students can understand, thus developing a fundamental awareness of systems that can be applied to increasingly advanced topics.

102. A: An important component in developing early elementary students' scientific inquiry skills is fostering their ability to formulate relevant predictions based upon observations and prior knowledge. This establishes the foundation for being able to craft testable hypotheses when designing and engaging in scientific investigations. "What if" questions encourage young children to think critically when approaching a problem because they must apply background knowledge to new information to make a logical prediction. In this example specifically, asking students what they think might happen if ice is left on the counter requires them to use what they already know about water and temperature to consider possible outcomes, thus prompting them to make a reasonable prediction.

103. B: Effectively differentiating science instruction includes incorporating activities that provide the appropriate level of challenge to align with the intellectual abilities of gifted and talented learners. Doing so sustains these students' engagement in scientific learning while promoting continuous development at a pace that corresponds with their individual needs. Differentiation for gifted and talented learners can be achieved through a variety of strategies, such as extending the scope of instruction, adding a layer of complexity to a summative assessment, or allowing for flexibility to explore personal interests. In this example, the teacher can accommodate gifted and talented students in the classroom by having them research local weather patterns throughout history. Such an activity would provide enrichment by allowing these students to explore the topic on a broader scale, identify long-term weather patterns, and ultimately gain a deeper understanding of occurring and recurring patterns in nature.

104. D: Providing young children with opportunities to self-assess as they participate in scientific inquiry is beneficial in fostering continuous learning and development. Doing so allows students to take ownership over their learning, thus increasing overall engagement and encouraging further scientific exploration. Self-assessment practices prompt students to monitor their own progress, identify personal strengths and areas for improvement, and recognize the need for support. Incorporating color-coded cards into learning activities for students to communicate their level of understanding is a highly effective self-assessment technique. This strategy requires students to continuously evaluate their own performances as they engage in scientific investigation and determine the need for additional assistance to be successful in achieving learning targets.

105. B: Early childhood students develop scientific knowledge and skills through hands-on learning experiences that foster their natural sense of curiosity and inquiry. Educators can facilitate this by incorporating realistic, age-appropriate scientific tools into learning experiences that encourage active exploration. Doing so helps young children build an understanding that in science, specific tools are utilized for gathering information and investigating new concepts, and it also promotes engagement by allowing students to physically interact with learning materials. By prekindergarten, most students should be able to properly utilize a hand magnifier when engaging in scientific learning. Placing this item in a sensory bin filled with rocks, sand, pebbles, and soil prompts students to closely examine the materials and identify differences for greater understanding of the concept that Earth is composed of various forms of matter.

106. A: Young children build knowledge and skills in science through developmentally appropriate experiences that demonstrate the prevalence of major scientific concepts in daily life. Such experiences meet students where they are in terms of ability, and they place learning in an immediately applicable context for increased relevancy, engagement, and understanding. Placing trash items found on the school playground into a bin of water and watching as it becomes increasingly dirty illustrates the negative impact of litter on students' surrounding environment, thus establishing a foundation for grasping this concept on a larger scale.

107. C: Building students' foundational understanding of basic scientific principles is essential to ensuring they have the tools necessary for approaching increasingly advanced concepts. Doing so provides students with a framework of reference from which to apply knowledge for continuous scientific learning and development. In this situation, implementing a project in which students construct a suitable habitat for a frog is an effective strategy for demonstrating that living things must have their needs met to survive. To be successful in this project, students must first have a fundamental awareness that all living things require food, water, shelter, and space. With this information in mind, students can begin to brainstorm what to include in the frog habitat, calculate the appropriate amount of space, and effectively plan the necessary steps for creating a suitable, functioning habitat that meets its survival needs.

108. D: Activities that demonstrate abstract scientific concepts through concrete learning experiences are beneficial in building students' foundational knowledge for continuous development. Such activities demonstrate the prevalence of seemingly complex scientific ideas in daily life, thus making learning relevant and accessible for greater overall understanding. The notion that Earth rotates on its axis every 24 hours, for example, may be initially difficult for young children to grasp. Having students trace one another's shadows at varying times throughout the day is an effective strategy for placing this concept in an age-appropriate and immediately applicable context. In doing so, students are prompted to notice the changing location of their shadows, thus fostering further inquiry and promoting a fundamental understanding that the position of Earth in relation to the Sun changes as the day progresses.

109. A: Students that have a strong foundational knowledge of the morphology of words are more effectively able to understand and acquire academic language. For science instruction specifically, this skill enables students to break down complex terms by identifying affixes and root words to determine their definitions. In this example, reviewing the morphology of the words "renewable" and "nonrenewable" would be helpful in promoting students' ability to comprehend the meaning of and distinguish between the two types of resources. Showing students that the words "renewable" and "nonrenewable" share the root word "new" and the suffix "-able," meaning "capable of," but that the prefixes "re-" and "non-" mean "again" and "not," respectively, helps them grasp that renewable resources can be replenished whereas nonrenewable resources cannot. Ensuring students can differentiate between these definitions at the beginning of the unit will be beneficial in establishing a framework of reference for building greater understanding of the concept.

110. B: Instilling the importance of producing and relying upon verifiable evidence is an essential component in building students' skills for applying the scientific method when engaging in inquiry. This includes teaching students that valid scientific experiments produce the same results when replicated under the same conditions, and that scientists typically repeat experiments several times to determine the reliability of data collected. Having students reproduce their own experiments in the classroom encourages them to think like scientists and apply these concepts to their own learning. In doing so, students build an understanding of how to produce and support their claims with verifiable evidence when communicating the findings of their scientific investigations.

111. C: Incorporating a unit on integrated pest management techniques into the early childhood science curriculum is beneficial in deepening students' understanding of the environment, ecological systems, and the ways in which both can be negatively impacted. This includes teaching young children that plants, animals, insects, and other organisms are considered pests when they exist in unwanted areas and have the potential to cause harm, and that when this occurs, their population must be controlled. Teachers can strengthen students' knowledge of these concepts first by teaching them what causes an organism to be classified as a pest, namely, how harmful and prevalent it is in the ecosystem in question. Pests are generally pervasive and harmful to the environment or other organisms in the area. After teaching how to identify an organism as a pest, it would subsequently be helpful to educate them on the habitats and survival needs of pests during such a unit. Doing so would help students build an understanding of the role of pests in their natural environment and the conditions that make certain locations hospitable. It would also help students brainstorm effective strategies for controlling pests in unwanted areas.

Health

112. A: Students' knowledge of and attitudes toward health and fitness are significantly shaped by imitating the actions, behaviors, and beliefs of the adults in their immediate environment. As lifelong habits begin in early childhood, it is important to model and encourage healthy choices, including eating nutritious foods and engaging in physical exercise, both inside and outside of the classroom. For several reasons, however, students' families may be unsure of ways to incorporate such practices into their daily lives or lack awareness of the importance of doing so. By providing information, resources, and suggestions related to health and fitness, teachers can involve families in the learning process and educate them on ways to reinforce these concepts at home. Extending health and fitness education outside of the classroom is beneficial in promoting students' positive attitudes toward wellness and establishing the foundation for adopting and maintaining good habits throughout their lives.

113. C: Most fine motor skills are acquired naturally, but teachers can support young children in their development by incorporating opportunities for practice throughout daily instruction. Implementing activities that encourage students to utilize their hands, wrists, and fingers to control tools and manipulate small objects helps them build muscle strength, hand-eye coordination, and dexterity. In this example, having students use tongs to move and place counting chips prompts them to employ small hand movements to properly utilize a tool, thus integrating an opportunity to develop this fine motor skill into mathematics instruction.

114. C: According to the Centers for Disease Control and Prevention (CDC), childhood obesity is defined as having a body mass index (BMI) at or above the 95th percentile. Obesity rates in young children have increased in recent years and are strongly correlated with several short- and long-term negative health consequences. Children that suffer from obesity often experience developmental difficulties across various domains, including limited ability to engage in physical activity, impaired cognition, and social and emotional harm. Further, individuals that are obese in childhood are more likely to remain so as adults and are at risk for serious health complications, such as diabetes, bone and joint issues, high blood pressure, and cardiovascular disease. Lifestyle factors such as poor nutrition, excess calories, and lack of exercise have been identified as some of the greatest contributors to childhood obesity. Early education and emphasis on the importance of health and wellness can be highly effective in helping to prevent childhood obesity. This includes teaching young children how to make responsible food choices, incorporating movement into daily learning experiences, modeling positive attitudes toward health and physical activity, and communicating with families about ways to reinforce these concepts at home. In doing so, teachers can encourage and instill practices within students that can become lifelong habits for maintaining health, fitness, and overall wellness.

115. A: Students gain a greater understanding of the importance of good nutrition when they learn the specific roles of food in keeping the body healthy. By second grade, most students have knowledge of the various food groups and can begin categorizing foods based upon characteristics such as healthy or unhealthy, high or low in fats and sugars, or their function in supporting different parts of the body. Having students sort pretend foods as they relate to various body parts provides a developmentally appropriate active learning experience in which students can visualize how food choices are relevant in maintaining overall health. Such an activity is beneficial in promoting students' internalization of this concept and encourages them to adopt healthy food habits in their daily lives.

116. C: Developing students' awareness of their own bodies is essential to promoting healthy lifestyle choices and habits. This includes teaching young children how to identify and describe the roles of major body parts and organs and the importance of maintaining physical health. Doing so helps students build knowledge of how different parts of the body work together and healthy practices for taking care of themselves. Having students label major body parts and organs on tracings of one another places these concepts in a hands-on, developmentally appropriate context in which students can visualize and physically identify each part of the body. Such an activity fosters their initial understanding of the location of major body parts and organs, thus establishing a foundation for learning how each one functions.

117. D: Incorporating opportunities for movement throughout the curriculum and into daily learning experiences is beneficial in promoting positive attitudes toward health and fitness. Students that are encouraged to participate in physical activity throughout the school day are more inclined to do so on their own. Brain breaks refer to a temporary pause in instruction in which students are prompted to engage in a movement activity with the intention of helping them refocus attention, reduce stress, and process learning. This versatile strategy can be differentiated to align with students' needs, interests, and preferences, and it promotes stronger connections to learning through movements that activate both sides of the brain by crossing the midline (movements in which the individual reaches across the body). In addition to its academic benefits, implementing a brain break into daily instruction is a highly effective method for incorporating physical activity into all areas of learning alongside the general health and fitness curriculum.

118. B: Teaching young children to recognize and respond appropriately in emergency situations is essential to developing their knowledge of how to protect their physical safety and health. This includes helping students learn their personal identifying information, such as their names, addresses, and phone numbers, as well as situations in which they may need to share it. Doing so in advance promotes emergency response preparedness as students will be more likely to remember this information in the event they become lost or separated during a stressful emergency situation. Teachers can incorporate multiple opportunities to practice this skill throughout daily learning activities, such as having students write their names, addresses, and phone numbers as part of a letter and number formation lesson in language arts.

119. C: Incorporating movement activities into daily instruction strengthens early childhood students' connections to learning while promoting positive attitudes toward health and fitness. When implementing such activities, however, teachers must follow specific precautions and guidelines in relation to student safety. The physical arrangement of the classroom should facilitate ease of movement, provide ample space to do so, and allow the teacher to easily access, monitor, and assist students as necessary. Teachers should also designate a specific area of the classroom for engaging in movement activities. Furniture, desks, and other large equipment should be situated away from this area to reduce the risk of student injury. Thoughtfully considering the physical arrangement of the classroom prior to implementing movement activities helps to provide students with a safe and orderly space to actively engage in learning.

120. D: Perceptual awareness allows individuals to simultaneously utilize sensory and physical motor skills when interacting with the environment. These skills are categorized as body awareness, spatial awareness, directional awareness, and temporal awareness, with each relating to a specific aspect of perceiving movement. Temporal awareness refers to one's ability to comprehend movement in relation to time and is necessary for performing a range of gross and fine motor activities. Students that have developed a sense of temporal awareness are able to notice differences or changes in speed, understand varying lengths of time, and demonstrate appropriate reaction times. By second grade, most students should have developed a degree of accuracy when catching objects that are kicked or thrown in their direction. While temporal awareness skills are often acquired naturally, students in this age group that struggle to do so would benefit from opportunities for additional practice. Continued difficulty, however, may suggest a potential developmental delay and would indicate the need for further evaluation of the student's abilities.

121. C: Students will inevitably arrive in the classroom with a diverse range of lifestyle habits, physical abilities, and interests. Promoting positive attitudes toward health and fitness includes recognizing these differences and aligning learning targets accordingly. One strategy for achieving this is to allow students to set personal health and fitness goals based upon their current skill levels. Completing health inventories will help students identify strengths and areas for growth to develop an individual plan for continuous improvement. Further, teachers can utilize the feedback from these inventories for differentiating health and fitness instruction to accommodate varying needs and preferences. Through this approach, students will build confidence as they develop skills and witness their own progress, thus encouraging them to continue improving upon their health and physical fitness.

122. B: Gross motor skills are those which allow individuals to engage in large-muscle movements that incorporate the use of the whole body, such as throwing, kicking, catching, jumping, or running. These skills are necessary for healthy physical development as well as for performing a variety of daily tasks. Therefore, multiple opportunities for practice should be incorporated in the early childhood classroom. While there are general characteristics associated with each age group in terms of gross motor skill development, young children will ultimately progress at varying rates. When planning physical activities, it is important that teachers recognize these differences and implement the appropriate accommodations, supports, and modifications for meeting students' individual needs. In this example, varying the sizes and weights of the balls as students practice throwing, catching, and kicking is an effective strategy for accommodating differences in strength, coordination, and balance. In doing so, the teacher meets students where they are in terms of ability and incorporates the appropriate amount of challenge for different skill levels to foster continuous improvement. Differentiating gross motor skill activities to align with students' developmental levels is beneficial in building students' confidence in their abilities and promoting positive attitudes toward physical activity.

123. D: In terms of physical fitness, balance refers to one's ability to demonstrate bodily control and stability while engaging in both locomotor and non-locomotor movements and stationary poses using a combination of muscle strength, vision, the vestibular system, and the proprioceptive system. As balance is a necessary component to building gross motor skills and performing a range of daily activities, assessing students' abilities in this area is necessary to ensure proper development, identify areas of individual need, and recognize a potential delay or disability. By first grade, students can be expected to exhibit enough balance and coordination to walk forward and backward on a balance beam. Students that are unable to do so would benefit from opportunities for additional practice to develop this skill. Continued difficulty, however, may suggest a potential disability or developmental delay that would indicate the need for further evaluation.

124. A: Manipulative movement skills refer to one's ability to engage in coordinated, purposeful bodily movements to control an object. Examples include actions that require the use of gross motor skills, such as kicking, throwing, or dribbling a ball, as well as those that incorporate fine motor abilities, such as drawing, tracing, or building a block tower. Manipulative movement skills are integral for healthy physical and cognitive development because they enable young children to explore and learn about the world around them and perform a range of necessary daily tasks. As these skills are applicable in a variety of contexts, teachers can implement multiple opportunities for practicing throughout daily learning experiences and across the early childhood curriculum.

125. D: For meaningful instruction that encourages continued interest in health and wellness, learning must be relevant to students' needs, interests, abilities, and specifically, cultural backgrounds. It is therefore important that teachers learn about the foods typically eaten by students in their classroom and incorporate them into lessons on nutrition, food groups, and healthy choices. This can be achieved by strategies such as displaying images of foods from various countries, having students sort familiar foods according to specific categories, and including pretend versions into play kitchen areas in the classroom. When students see their diversity reflected in instruction, learning becomes inclusive and applicable as they see where the foods they eat daily fit into nutrition instruction, thus fostering personal connections that promote positive attitudes toward health and fitness.

126. A: Locomotor skills are those which enable one to move the body in a particular direction to get from one location to another. Examples include running, walking, skipping, hopping, and leaping. Development of locomotor skills in early childhood is essential for building the strength, coordination, and bodily and spatial awareness necessary for engaging in physical activities and performing a variety of daily tasks. As young children learn best through active play opportunities, implementing group games that require the use of a range of locomotor movements, such as tag, follow the leader, and hopscotch, provides an engaging, developmentally appropriate setting for building these skills.